D1286493

# THE ART OF BEING TOGETHER

## Common Sense for Lifelong Relationships

Francis H. Wade

FORWARD MOVEMENT
CINCINNATI, OHIO

Second Printing 2007
Cover design: Robert W. Grove
Layout: Carole Miller
Printed in Canada

 Forward Movement
300 West Fourth Street
Cincinnati, Ohio 45202-2666

©2005, 2007 Forward Movement

www.forwardmovement.org

To Mary

With seven daffodils

# Contents

# INTRODUCTION

COMMON SENSE about marriage is something of a contradiction in terms these days. So few people seem to be able to make sense of the working parts of matrimony that it is nowhere near common. The divorce rate is close to 50 percent, and the failure rate of marriage that does not express itself in divorce must be much higher. But there are some basic principles that are almost always present in successful marriages and seldom at work in failed ones. Married persons who want to strengthen their relationship and those considering marriage could profit from reflection on them. You have in your hand an attempt to set some of those principles before you for thought and discussion. You may reasonably wonder why this writer thinks he has found that which has proven so elusive for others. The answer is, basically, that I have had a good seat for watching people struggle to achieve harmony in their homes, and I have learned a few things.

I have been an Episcopal priest since 1966 and have served in congregations the entire time. It is a work that I dearly love for many reasons, not least of which is the time I get to spend with people as they go through great and critical moments in life. People have honored me by asking that I be with them as they wrestled with growing up, being a friend, being in love, getting married. I have been privileged to work with people who were giving up on a relationship and others who were considering giving up on life itself. I have been with families as they dealt with difficult children, difficult parents, and difficult times. There have been addictions, accidents, infidelities, abuses, and illnesses; some wonderful triumphs over incredible odds and some tragic failures in the face of unnecessary obstacles. I have seen good people simply blown away from what they wanted most in life, and I have seen some pretty shabby people get along better than I thought they deserved.

All of us struggle to be human in some positive way, even those who seem to be the least interested and most obstinate. All of us try to do a good job of being a son or daughter, a friend or a spouse. Many of us do not seem to have much equipment—skill, tact, heart, or experience—to apply to the effort, but I have never met anyone who did not want to live harmoniously with others. I will admit that I have been privy to some bizarre notions of what harmony would look like, but everyone has wanted harmony. In addition, I have been married since 1963 and have experienced many of the same joys and sorrows as my friends and readers. Over the years I have observed, experienced, blundered into, had pointed out, and have figured out the principles set forth in this volume.

My observations tell me there are some principles about being together that apply across the board. The principles are not complex, but they seem to be important to a shared life. The particular focus here is marriage, but the principles (with slight adjustments) are part of any kind of relationship that people are willing to work on to keep.

My perspective is that of a Christian. It is my tradition and the way I make sense out of life. The fact that I am a believer is basic to who I am and cannot be screened from my observations or reflections. Yet the principles set forth in this volume are applicable to life, not just the life of faith. It is not my purpose to convince the reader of the value of belief in general, much less my Christian beliefs in particular. The reader will, I hope, grant that most of our basic understandings of human relationships were forged in the Judeo-Christian tradition. Many, if not most, of our fundamental images for living with others come from it, and its precepts still help us to identify healthy and unhealthy relationships. There is faith and there are images of faith in this work, but those looking for or dreading a "Christian perspective" on marriage will be disappointed—or relieved—depending on where they are coming from.

One of the prime motivations behind this book is the need for persons about to be married to establish a firm foundation for their life together. If people are wed at the age of thirty they can anticipate more than half a century of shared living. The principles and conduct that enable a relationship to last—much less grow and prosper—for that length of time are different from those that allowed relationships with roommates, siblings, coworkers, and neighbors to work. In addition to the impact of longevity on the institution of marriage, changes in society help to set the family begun today on a journey far different from that of previous generations. Gender roles that used to be fixed now must be negotiated. The proximity and interaction with parents and other elders is not what it is remembered to have been and the new family may be cut off from a source of wisdom, to say nothing of support.

Concepts of work, neighborhood, parenting, social responsibility, the sanctity of vows, and the acceptability of divorce are all up for discussion, if not up for grabs. These changes are not all bad. Some represent great strides toward the fullness of life. But the reader will have to admit that change—cultural, social, religious, personal, and individual—alters things. It changes human hearts and human relationships, too. The wisdom of the past cannot be uncritically applied to the future. People embarking on a life of commitment need new tools as well as traditional insights with which to make a solid foundation. And foundations for this sort of enterprise are made of far more than fondness and common interests. It is my hope the principles set forth here will provide the basis for long and productive talks for those approaching marriage.

The second motivation behind this work is to address relationships that hurt. Marriages are like people. They need nurture and care. They need to be educated and allowed to mature. Like people they have aches and pains, experience accidents, and sometimes are seriously ill. During such times a little help may come in handy. This book is intended to be read and used by people whose basic need is the ability to talk to one another. Such conversations may need a jump-start, a way of understanding, a way out of the circular and repetitive thinking that occupies troubled people on their pillows at night. It is not uncommon for one person to feel there is a problem when the other does not. It is difficult to have a productive conversation when one sees so clearly what the other cannot fathom, no matter how hard he or she tries. It is a dangerous time when one person wants, even needs, to renegotiate the relationship but the other cannot imagine a different way of life. The principles here may provide a basis for the conversation that will find the health that is hidden in every crisis.

It is important to remember that books do not have the power to save relationships; people do. Books can help, but the real work is to be done in conversation. In fact, the purpose of this book will not be satisfied if it is only read and not discussed. In relationships, what people say to one another, no matter how awkwardly, is infinitely more powerful than anything that is written, no matter how elegantly. This leads to one of the first principles of a shared life: *The hardest work of marriage is talking when you would rather not talk and listening when you would rather not listen.* Hopefully this book will give the readers some things to talk about, help in getting a new relationship off to a good start, some ways to make listening less of a chore, some ideas for making difficult conversations more productive, and a few suggestions for reducing the number and intensity of painful exchanges. To that end, each principle is preceded by a brief "Points of View" which sets forth some of the ways people might understand a situation differently. Most of the points are ones I have heard made in counseling sessions. They may not appear reasonable to you, but they seem that way to someone—and may seem so to your partner. After each principle is stated, there is a section called "Beginning to talk about…" These are questions that may help you to get a conversation going. They are there if you need them and should be ignored if you do not. As stated earlier, your conversation is what counts.

One additional note on conversations between men and women: In my experience, women are generally better than men in recognizing and expressing feelings.

The reasons for this may be born in us or perhaps it is taught to us. In either case it does not matter. If that generalization is true in your relationship, it means that when the focus is on feelings (and it often is in marriage), each of you is called upon to bring a different kind of patience to the discussions.

People who see life in terms of thoughts and actions will need to develop new understandings of the importance of emotions that previously were unexplored, ignored, or denied. This is not done quickly or easily.

Those who have a ready appreciation of the importance of feelings will need to avoid the temptation to use that facility to quickly "win," or to require that the conversation be entirely on their terms.

I remember talking with a couple who had serious communication problems. As we sat in my office, she poured out her soul speaking of loneliness, disappointment, and frustration in her marriage experience. As she spoke, the body language of her husband indicated that he was very uncomfortable with such a display. In his mind (we later determined), strong people are not pushed around by their emotions. "You just suck it up and keep going," he said. His was a successful approach to the limited and tangible problems of life such as a sprained ankle or a lost promotion, but it brought little to the limitless and intangible concerns of human relationships. With his attitude toward emotion, he had developed no skills in identifying his own or an ability in responding to hers. He needed to learn a new language before they could talk at any depth about their life together. They both needed to give the other unique gifts of patience and effort as that preliminary process went on. It was a difficult task for them both.

Neither this book, nor any other, will keep being together from being difficult. The basic principles of sharing life are simple. But simple is not the same thing as easy. People have to work to be in loving relationships. The work, however, is worth it. Being together, sharing a commitment, trusting and being trusted, building a relationship and feeling it deepen and broaden are among the greatest joys in life. These are the things that make life worthwhile, and they are what this book is about.

# THE BASICS

# The purpose of marriage is to make life better.

## *Points of View*

A. Marriage is not necessary…It is just a lot of social baggage. A former celebrity divorced his wife of twenty-six years saying he no longer needed the social prop of marriage…Most marriages in this country do not work (49.7 percent of marriages in the United States end in divorce)…I have been married before and I do not want to go through that kind of pain again…We don't need it. We have a fine relationship now. Why take a chance on messing it up?…The one food that is guaranteed to kill sexual appetite is wedding cake. If it ain't broke, why fix it?…We should not be pressured by our families or society. It is just our business, no one else's.

B. Relationships need to move forward, they cannot stay in one place. The next step for us is marriage…I admit that I like the "social baggage" that comes with a wedding. I do not care what it means to my family or society, it means something to me. It marks a turning point in life, a milestone…Our relationship is not like any other. The statistics do not describe us...I am not like your first husband. You cannot hold us a prisoner to the way he behaved...We need a sense of rootedness and permanence in our relationship, a foundation to build on...If we have children they deserve a legal family...The divorce rate is actually declining (down 1.3% between 1986 and 1997) and in communities that require premarital training the rate is down as much as 35%...What does a celebrity's life have to do with us? And, if by some stretch of imagination it does, why did he get married again in 1999?

## *Principle*

The simple fact is that marriage does not *do* anything. The days when our social conventions made marriage and children a necessity for the validation of females and highly recommended for proof of maturity among males are gone in most places and fading in the rest. Neither men nor women have to be married to be granted a responsible role in the community. The world around us still expects marriage but no longer requires it. More and more couples are living together without bothering to include marriage vows in their arrangement. People are beginning to see that marriage does not actually *do* anything, and they are wondering why one would want to be married at all.

The answer is that marriage can make life better. That was the original idea, and it continues to be the compelling reason for it. The Book of Genesis begins with stories that set forth the basics of our understandings about life. In the first and second chapters the creation stories are told. These stories give shape to our concept of marriage. The first is that creation is divided into two parts. The first part is what we call the natural order, that which runs on God's energy and is essential for sustaining life. It includes the earth, sun, planets, stars, vegetation, and animals, including human beings. All that is required for bearing fruit and providing for regeneration are established in this period. The natural order, which includes us, is judged to be "good." Indeed, it is determined to be "very good." Marriage is not part of this phase of creation which means, by one account, that it is "good" to be single. The point is clearly allowed that marriage is not essential.

After the day of Sabbath rest, a new period of creation begins. This second phase of creation continues to the present and requires the energy of both God and humanity. It provides the establishment of morality and ethics, governments and society, theology and faith, personal growth and community development. It is, as all expressions of history would attest, an awkward process. God and people work together like dancers who are hearing different music. It is in this difficult period that marriage appears. According to Genesis, marriage is the first product of the mutual creation of God and people, and it grows out of the first negative notion in the Bible. In Genesis 2:18 God observes, "It is not good that the man should be alone; I will make him a helper as his partner." After some dabbling and experimentation, the result is Eve. Lest we get bogged down in some worn-out theories of the superiority of males over females, we need to take a moment to note that the word *Adam* is an ancient Semitic term for "people" or "society." It is generic and does not mean males. *Eve* is a word which basically means "source" and in this context refers to "life source" or "birth." The story of the creation of Eve is about families, not females. It grows out of the sense that "it is not good to be alone" and moves to the conclusion that life will be better if people are together. That is the basic premise of marriage. People's concepts of what it takes to make life better has changed many times over the years. But the basic point has not.

It may seem a little dated or naive to base the principles of a modern relationship on such an ancient story. But that old story is still current. Almost every married couple I know include something like the Genesis story in the account of their own relationship. Someone, at some point, concluded that it was no longer good to be alone and that life would be better if the two were together. That fresh, romantic, and exciting idea is essentially a reenactment of the second chapter of Genesis.

The business of marriage then is to make a life together that is better than life apart. From that simple truth comes the basic task of each partner in a marriage. It is to do all in your power to see to it that your partner's life is better because you are part of it. That is your role in the pit of your worst disagreement and at the summit of your greatest passion. When two people have as their primary question, "How can I make your life better?", their relationship can only soar. When only one, or neither, is motivated by that question, very little soaring and probably a lot of souring is likely. You may rightly say that people can make such a promise to one another without being married, but don't stop with that. The next section is about commitment and how it creates wonderful opportunities for a relationship. Marriage is a special form of commitment. Work on these questions and then take a look at what commitment can mean.

## *Beginning to talk about marriage:*

Where did you learn about marriage? From your parents? Neighbors? Extended family? Television or movies?

What did you learn from them?

Do you still believe those lessons are true? Are they true about this relationship?

What are the strengths and weaknesses of this relationship?

What would make your life better?

How could we make each other's lives better? (The author's list is in the section titled "Why Bother?" Don't peek unless you have to. Your list is what is important.)

## PRINCIPLE TWO

# Commitment is the key.

### Points of View

A. I am ready to settle down...I want a solid foundation from which to face the changes and challenges of life...I want to be with you and I am ready to say so. I want to live with a plural "we" instead of a singular "I"...I know that making a commitment has risks, but living without commitment has risks, too...I know that I do not know what the future will hold; I never will. I do know that I want to face that future with you in my life...I want a commitment from you, and the only way to get it is for me to make a commitment to you.

B. Commitment is a loss of freedom...What if we stop loving one another?...I am not into traditional roles of wife and husband...We cannot make a commitment about a future we do not know. Things change. People change...I am just not ready to make a commitment. There are still things I want to do before I settle down...I just do not feel ready...You should not be stuck with me if you no longer want me...I want the freedom to be able to pack up and go if I want to.

# *Principle*

Commitment is the bond created when two people choose one another. Each must make the choice individually, but there is no commitment if it is only made by one. Where one makes a commitment and the other makes something less, the relationship is uneven—like a table with a short leg or a car out of alignment. They can function, but not as they were intended. Commitment is what "love" means in marriage. "Love" is a very overworked word in our language. It is used to describe the way we relate to God, country, family, our favorite music, certain foods, the clothing we covet, and the people we marry. Obviously the word means different things depending on the context. In the context of marriage it means commitment.

Unfortunately the word "commitment" does not have a lot of romantic, sexy, or even emotional connotations. Please do not think that a married relationship should be without those feelings. They are enormously important from the honeymoon cottage to the nursing home. But a longterm relationship cannot rely on feelings to provide the kind of foundation it needs. Feelings come and go in fact as well as intensity. Commitment remains. It is the bond between people that is strong enough to carry all of their feelings back and forth between them. It allows people to share great passion and real anger. It permits surprises as well as disappointments. It has room for good feelings and bad, conversation and quiet, being alone and being together, confidence and confusion, fear and joy, vulnerability and generosity. Commitment can tolerate bad days, bad moods, bad decisions, and bad consequences. It always has a capacity for forgiveness, recovery, celebration, renewal, and fun. Commitment includes every feeling known to life, but it is deeper than feeling. That is how it gives character and definition to lifelong relationships.

It is obviously not something "to be entered into lightly," but neither is it to be feared. I have talked with many who were reluctant to make a commitment of this kind because they only understood it in negative terms. They saw commitment as a loss of options, a loss of freedom. It is true that some possibilities are set aside when commitments are made. But they are like the loss of childhood as one grows up, or the loss of a piece of a dream when one career is chosen over another. Commitment is not a simple loss of freedom: It is choosing one kind of freedom over another. There is a special kind of life found inside of commitment that is unlike what one experiences outside of it. In a committed relationship there is opportunity to explore the intimate depths of life. Instead of the freedom to change partners one has the chance to share the changes in one partner and to face the changes of life with one partner. Inside of commitment the future can be tested and tasted. The energy that used to go into questions like "How are we doing?" can be devoted to deeper issues like "What are we doing and what will we do?" For those who have the courage to be vulnerable, there is unending discovery in the sharing of thoughts, dreams, ideas, and hopes. Inside of commitment there is freedom to rely on the good will of another, to think out loud, to be forgiven, to be generous. You may note that these things are possible in any relationship, and I must agree. The point is degree and intensity. It is like the difference between being a Boy Scout and being in the army, being a passenger in an airplane and being the pilot, studying for a test and taking one, thinking and speaking, hoping and seeking.

It is clear that not everyone can or should make marriage commitments. When the commitment is forced or made with a sense of resignation there is not likely to be enough glue to last a lifetime. When the commitment *is* made, it should be made in the confidence the prize is clearly worth the cost. The freedoms of being *un*committed are quite different from those found in commitment. Both have their pluses and minuses. The wise will think about them before choosing one path or another because the two kinds of freedom do not mix well.

While there is no simple way to know about when to enter into a commitment, there is a question that can help to clarify the situation. The question is: *If I make you the biggest influence in my life, will I become the kind of person I want to be?* That may sound selfish, but it is the most important question for those considering marriage. We can choose friends and dates by asking if we enjoy these people. That works well. Marriage, however, is different. It is about the rest of one's life and about a level of intimacy and sharing that are only faintly reflected in friendships and romances. Marriage is the single greatest determiner of the kind of person we will be. That is why the question mentioned above is so important. People who do not like themselves or sense that they are becoming someone they do not want to be have real trouble holding up their end of the marriage commitment. The sense that one is being abused or taken for granted, is becoming fearful or losing a sense of joy or fun about life, feeling left alone and neglected, or any of a thousand forms of negative self-perception—sets off alarm bells in a marriage. In my experience, people can live a long time without liking their partner, but begin to ask for help or think about divorce when they stop liking themselves.

Despite the price in personal freedom and the danger of personal disappointment, being in a committed relationship is absolutely the best place for living life. To know and be known, to be trustworthy and be trusted, to actively seek that which is best for one who is actively seeking that which is best for you, to give to one who is giving to you, to be able to think openly and speak freely, to share memories as well as dreams, consequences as well as plans, to reach for one who is reaching for you, to listen to one who wants your ear, to love and be loved—is to know that the primitive notion of life being better when people are together was a pretty good idea.

## *Beginning to talk about commitment:*

Think of four or five words that you would like for those who know you best to use when they describe you. These words represent what you most want to be. Remember that *being* is different from *doing*. This is not about careers, but character.

How does this relationship support and/or hinder you as you try to become the kind of person you hope to be?

How does your partner influence your life?

What would intimacy in a relationship be like? What kind of freedom does it offer?

Why do you suppose people find intimacy scary?

Does the distinction between the freedom in commitment and the freedom from commitment make any sense at all?

What do you like about the most romantic song, movie, book, play, or poem you know?

## PRINCIPLE THREE

# Something significant happens in a wedding.

## Points of View

**A.** I do not care what is done in the wedding. Let's just get it over with and get on with our lives... Weddings are for women. If guys had anything to do in a wedding they would call it patrimony instead of matrimony. I will just do what I am told...Your parents are paying for it, let them decide...I want a wedding like Sally's. That was a real blast...Is your mother going to try to run our family the same way she is trying to run the wedding?...Do your friends have to get drunk at the reception?...Every time I ask what I can do to help, you say you "don't know." Then you are mad at me for not helping...Isn't this stupid?

**B.** This really means something. It is not just a ritual. We are saying something important about ourselves and the way we will live the rest of our lives. I want to know what we are doing and why...We need to respect what others want, but it is still *our* wedding... Photographer, flowers, dress, invitations, limousines, caterer, tuxedos, gifts, organist, candles, videographer, centerpiece, cake, parking, reception, stamps, musicians, guestbook, license, calligrapher, out of town guests, clergy, blood tests...Why are we doing all of this? Where did the meaning go?...Why don't you know what to do to be helpful?...This is supposed to be the greatest day in our lives and I just want it to be over...Isn't this exciting?

## *Principle*

A wedding is more than a social event, a photo op, a reason to party, or a prelude to a honeymoon—although, thankfully, it is all of those things, too. Something actually happens during a wedding. Things are different from what they were before. Being married is different from being in love, being engaged, living together, or from anything else in life. Some of the ways are explainable, most are not; but the difference is real and can only be missed by those determined not to be aware of it.

In a religious ceremony, the difference is acted out in very specific ways. When the couple say "In the name of God I take you to be my husband or wife," they are declaring God to be the owner of their relationship in the same way that explorers declare a nation to own a new land by claiming it "in the name of _____." When the officiant pronounces the couple to be husband and wife in the name of God, the community is affirming that God has accepted the couple's gift. The relationship between the two becomes something of God's. The word we use for such things is "holy." In the words of the final blessing, the relationship is given back to the new family as a sacred trust. So one of the things that happens in a wedding is that the relationship, which originally belonged to the couple, now belongs to God. Before the wedding they shared something like all other human relationships in that they determined the openness, character, honesty, level of caring and commitment, even the duration of their life together. Now that framework is no longer what the bride and groom might fashion, but what people over thousands of years have figured to be what God had in mind when we were called out of aloneness and into union. The couple does not have to invent or discover what makes life together better; they can rely on the wisdom of their ancestors. That wisdom is expressed in the marriage vows (see Principle Four).

A wedding is also a creative moment. Something is made during the ceremony, and that something is a family. The concepts of family have changed from age to age and society to society, but the importance of it is unchanged. It is and always has been one of God's greatest gifts to people as well as one of the most important building blocks of human community. It is worth the price of two coffees to sit down in some welcoming place and talk about what it means to be a family. What are its privileges and responsibilities? Its dangers and rewards? What kind of family do you want to be? Also consider that you are not becoming a family in isolation. There are nests of families. You are becoming a family that is (for better or for worse) connected to your families of origin as well as the extended family of in-laws, aunts, and cousins. You will need to figure out what that means and how you wish to relate to them. One by-product of the decisions you make about the wedding is that you will send a signal to your nest of families about how you want to relate to them. If you ignore their sensibilities (what does a heavy metal punk rock band at the reception say to your elders?) or fight over control (who gets to decide what?) or let them take over (everybody else knows best), you are establishing a pattern for future family relationships. Weddings are important family events, and the importance lives on long after the honeymoon is over.

In addition to all of this, a wedding is a civil ceremony. The importance of this aspect of the wedding is expressed in the mundane licensing process that is required. The civil contract represents the fact that society has a stake in the new family. Becoming a family includes taking a place in the community as well as the "nest of families." We have chosen to organize society with the family as one of the basic foundational blocks. Marriage is not a private matter; the license says it is not just "your business," but everybody's business. Weddings cannot take place without at least one witness and without a license from the community. The couple's private, intimate relationship is set into the larger context of the civil and (in most cases) the faith community. Clearly, it is still a private relationship. As long as the broader scope of law is maintained, it is no one's business how you function as a family. But we all have a stake in the kind of family you are. We need you to support one another in being a positive part of our common life as a taxpaying, recycling, law-abiding, child rearing, volunteering, smiling, and waving asset to the neighborhood. Your marriage license implies your agreement to do so.

Wedding and engagement rings give some indication of this private and public nature of marriage. The engagement ring is a symbol of the very personal relationship between the two. It is normally given and received with no one else around. The wedding ring represents the fact that this private relationship is being moved out into the larger arena of community. This love is taking its place on the family tree, under the law, and in the hands of God. Unlike engagement rings, wedding bands are given and received in front of God and everybody. That is the reason some faith traditions (mine included) traditionally bless wedding bands but not engagement rings. A blessing is a public act giving a definition or meaning to an object. The blessing of wedding rings makes them symbols of the fact that the relationship between these two people belongs to God. The meaning of that fact is lived out in the community. The specific meaning of the engagement ring is spelled out in the intimate life of the couple. It is none of the community's business. The wedding changes things by adding the public dimension of life to that which before was only private. It expresses that difference by adding the public wedding band to the private engagement ring.

Being married is fundamentally different from not being married. It may be the simple and glorious effect of choosing and being chosen; it may be basking in the love of all those friends and family members who gather to wish you well; it may be that something profound about life actually gets done. Perhaps there is something built into us that is turned loose by marriage. Maybe it is a time when the heart, mind, and soul come into step with one another. Probably it is when we can finally hear, feel, and know the word that God pronounced over all of life: "It is good, it is very good." Something significant happens in a wedding. If yours is not yet, expect it. If it has been done, stretch your memory to reclaim it. If you have a future with some one, care for it.

You will note that these comments about what happens in the wedding assume that it is primarily a religious ceremony with the civil contract executed on the side. That is not meant to diminish the importance of civil ceremonies themselves. If you do not believe in God, or if your concept of God does not include a Being interested enough in you to care what you promise to it, then have a civil ceremony and forget the religious part. I am speaking of non-belief, not simple doubt. All honest faith has doubt in it. If your choice is between a civil ceremony and a hypocritical one, choose the civil. This moment in your life is too important to be characterized by hypocrisy. Can you imagine telling the person you love that you will deal with him or her honestly and openly for the rest of your life and demonstrating it with an elaborate ceremony in which you say things you do not believe? I hope that you agree that the integrity of the foundation you lay at your wedding is more important than ritual or custom. Religion has no corner on integrity. If you are a non-believer, have the courage to act like one. If you come to religion later on, you can always have the marriage blessed. Be sure that what you say on your wedding day is as honest and faithful as you know how to be.

### *Beginning to talk about weddings:*

How do you feel about the "nest of families" we are joining?

What strengths do they offer us? What problems do they represent?

Is it hard for us to talk about each other's families of origin? Why?

Have we talked much about what we believe about God? What more can we say to each other about it?

What role do you see for God in our life together?

What do engagement and wedding rings mean to you? Why do you suppose women wear engagement rings and men do not?

What do you think is different about being married?

## PRINCIPLE FOUR

# Marriage vows are about the way people live together.

## *Points of View*

A. This relationship is just between us. What does God have to do with it?...We have just grown apart...Marrying a woman for her beauty makes as much sense as eating a bird for its singing.[1] But it is a common mistake nonetheless...You say you will but you never do. I need more than that...I don't have time for you right now...I'm OK and you're OK. What is the problem?... What can I do to help you? What can I do to make our life better?...I do not feel special to you anymore...Quit bugging me all of the time...You don't bring me flowers anymore.[2]

---

[1]Charles Frazier, *Cold Mountain* (New York: Vintage Contemporaries [division of Knopf Publishing Group], 1998).

[2]Neil Diamond and Alan and Marilyn Bergman, "You Don't Bring Me Flowers Anymore" lyrics (1991).

**B.** We just need to talk more...Did our marriage change your life or just add a wife to it?...When will you grow up and take some responsibility?...What happened to us that let him become so attractive to you?...What do you mean when you say you love me? I hear the words but do not see the meaning...There are only 24 hours in a day. We cannot make time for each other or for anything else. We are not talking about time but priority. We are not making each other a priority, and it is starving our relationship...This is forever, right? We have to work it out.

## *Principle*

It always amazes me that people in marriages do not realize that they have made some promises to one another and to God about the way they are going to live together. Most think that they have only promised to stick together ("till death do us part") and have no idea that they made some specific statements about how they will go about it. People are shocked to find that they made ten distinct statements during their wedding about how they will treat one another, and that their family and friends made two promises about how they will behave toward the couple. I am referring to the service that is set forth in *The Book of Common Prayer* in my own religious tradition. There are differences in other traditions, but the basic points are almost always the same.

### 1. To live together in the covenant of marriage:

Covenant means agreement. The agreement of marriage is not just between the two people but includes the community and, in a religious service, God. People who decide to live together have a covenant that is strictly between them. People who decide to get married are operating on a broader stage and have agreed to maintain a relationship with something greater than themselves. Marriages that turn inward become like people who turn inward—self-absorbed, fewer and fewer ideas about life, restricted supplies of refreshment, less to talk about, a loss of wonder and discovery, at best a mild form of depression. Marriages, and individuals, who keep a primary focus on that which is larger than themselves can expect a certain amount of confusion, but also a never ending supply of energy, hope, strength, and purpose.

## 2. To love:

Love in this context means commitment and it is discussed in Principle Two. The implication for day-to-day living is that the commitment of each needs to be regularly communicated to the other. Marriage is something two people do. If one person feels committed to another, but the other person is not reminded of it, the marriage can suffer. We are all forgetful about being loved and need to be reminded from time to time. Courtesy, good manners, thoughtfulness, surprises, support, compassion, conversation, and an effort to please that is responded to with gratitude, pleasure, reciprocation, and respect go a long way toward fulfilling this vow. Love is often supported by words such as "I thought you might enjoy…", "How can I help?", "I'm sorry…", "What do you think?", and even "I love you." It is amazing how soon such words can escape from a relationship often under the cover of the notion that actions speak louder than words. The assumption is that if I am doing what I said I would do and keeping the commitments I think I made, I do not have to say anything about it. While it is true that actions speak louder than words, it is also true that actions *and* words speak even louder. How did we get the idea that we had to choose between words and actions? Both are important to maintaining and growing a relationship.

### 3. To comfort:

Comfort is an old word that means to "be a source of strength." The place we hear it used this way in modern times is in the definition of treason, which is "to provide aid and comfort to the enemy." It does not mean providing cookies and milk for terrorists; it means being a source of strength to them and their cause. In marriage it means knowing what your partner is trying to do in life and what kind of strength your spouse needs to accomplish it. His or her issues will probably not be your own. What challenges or frightens, what threatens or excites, what is rewarding or frustrating, difficult or compelling to your spouse may not be the same for you. Comforting requires some sense of what your partner is doing and what it takes for him or her to do it. Otherwise the strength we try to provide may not be appropriate to what is really going on. How many times have we thought we were helping and others thought we were no help at all? This promise, like most of the others, is made much easier by honest conversation.

### 4. To honor:

Honor means simply to take one another seriously. It includes such basic acts of engagement as listening, thinking, caring, disagreeing, sharing, reflecting, and planning. None of these activities is especially difficult nor do they require large blocks of time and energy. Perhaps that is why we have trouble remembering their importance.

We often hear of couples who "just grew apart." In coffee break and cocktail party language it means that nobody did anything obvious. No one was in anyone else's bed, nobody was beat up, and the rent money was not gambled away. The implication is that no marriage vows were broken; it was something that just happened and it was not anybody's fault. That kind assessment, however, is generally wrong. The marriage vow that is broken when people "just grow apart" is the promise to honor one another. People who take one another seriously and are engaged in one another's lives might fight like cats and dogs, but they do not "just grow apart." People grow apart when they forget, or fail, to do the simple day-to-day task of being involved in one another's life. That is what honoring means.

## 5. To keep:

This means keeping one's side of the bargain. If you said you would be home at 6:00 p.m., then be home at 6:00 p.m. If you said you would pick up a loaf of bread and a quart of milk, do it. If you said all was forgiven, don't bring it up again. If you cannot do what you promised, admit it, explain it, and do better the next time. Keeping promises in a marriage is what stands between a healthy relationship and one that is plagued with a crippling sense of being taken for granted. If the office or the offspring, the hobby or the house, parents or partners, television or the team seem always to take precedence over the promises between you, a deadly virus is making its way into the marriage. The promise maker rarely sees the situation the same way as the promise receiver. The maker almost always sees the failure as an isolated incident. The receiver tends to see it as part of a series or a pattern. It does not matter who is right. Perception is the cut that lets the virus in. If one feels consistently on the short end of the other's priorities and promises, the virus is in and needs to be taken seriously by both. It may mean that promises need to be spelled out more clearly. The difference between a possibility and a promise is sometimes missed in casual conversation. It may mean that expectations need to be adjusted, new efforts need to be made, priorities reordered, sensitivities sharpened, or realities discovered. The simple wedding promise "to keep" is connected to the thousands of promises that knit the marriage together.

## 6. To forsake all others:

This vow means two things. The first is what everybody knows it means—staying out of other people's beds. But there is much more than that. To understand the greater meaning, we need to know something about adultery and why almost every culture that treats marriage as a good thing views adultery as a bad thing. The reason is that marriages, in any culture or time, are subject to a great deal of pressure and stress. We are very different from one another. Georgetown University professor Deborah Tannen, in her book, *You Just Don't Understand*,[3] makes the point that conversation between men and women is cross-cultural, the basic assumptions about life

---

[3] Deborah Tanner, *You Just Don't Understand: Women and Men in Conversation* (New York: Harper Collins, 2001).

are different. We may think we were made for each other but we were not. Each of us is an individual and no two of us fit perfectly together. In addition to the internal stresses of our differences there are significant pressures from outside the relationship. Bills must be paid, children make demands, families and friends are sometimes a problem, careers require sacrifices, the lawn needs mowing, and so on. Because marriage is subject to so much tension the bond between the two people must be protected and strengthened. Commitment, conversation, sharing, and other things help to make the bond stronger.

One of the greatest sources of strength to the marriage bond is the sexual relationship between the partners. Its intimacy, vulnerability, opportunities for generosity and sharing, fun, and play all help to forge a deep and powerful connection in a marriage. The problem with adultery is that it weakens that bond by violating the covenant. The deception of adultery can make open and honest sexual response impossible. It forces the sexual relationship out of the warmth of deep intimacy into the tepid shallowness of performance. When partners enter into sexual intimacy with a person outside the marriage, whether they get caught or not, they weaken that bond. Other terrible things can be associated with adultery, but the basic problem is what it does to that all-important connection and covenant between husband and wife.

If one can accept that adultery is wrong primarily because it weakens the marriage bond, then one can see that there are other relationships that are not sexual which can have the same effect. It is possible to be caught up in "emotional adultery" that is asexual.

The two most common partners in emotional adultery are careers and children. It is possible to get so wrapped up in them that the effect is to weaken the marriage. I have also worked with marriages where the emotionally adulterous relationship focused on parents, volunteerism, sports, friends, pets, even prayer and meditation.

The solution is not to avoid interest in other people or activities. Remember that the covenant of marriage includes a healthy engagement with the wider world. The possibility of physical adultery need not keep one from having close relationships with members of the opposite sex. Nor should the possibility of emotional adultery keep one from developing compelling interests, demanding responsibilities, or important friendships. The solution is to integrate those relationships into the life of the marriage. If you have lunch with an attractive person and hold in the back of your mind the hope that your spouse does not find out about it, that is adulterous, divisive, and destructive whether anything happens or not. The idea in the back of your mind is weakening the marriage by its secrecy. On the other hand, if at the end of the day when you get home you talk about the fine time you had with your lunch partner, there is no adultery. The event is integrated into the marriage. If you tell your partner about this enjoyable lunch and the response is anger, suspicion, or accusations, that partner is producing the effect of adultery by preventing the healthy integration of the event. The same dynamic, the same importance of integrating experiences, applies to working late, playing golf, time with friends, visits to your mother, or any other aspect of life that could be important to you. The involvement is fine if it can be integrated into the marriage. Indeed, it can make the marriage richer. But if it cannot be talked about at home, no matter who finds it impossible to do so, it functions as emotional adultery. It is, as in almost all aspects of marriage, a two-way street having to do with what is said and how it is responded to.

Fidelity, then, is staying out of other people's beds; but it is more than that. It is bringing the stories, people, events, and ideas of your day home to be shared. And it is listening to those stories in a trusting and affirming manner. Fidelity is not just about something we avoid doing. It is about something we work to do on a daily basis.

### 7.  To have and to hold:

This vow speaks to one of the most common and dangerous traps in marriage. It has to do with the patterns and routines of the shared life. The trap is when one assumes that the pattern is fine and the other finds it restrictive or unrewarding. The terms most often used by those who fall into the trap are "suffocating" or "ignored."

Having and holding another person is about how much time you spend together and how much private space each needs. It is the scope, depth, and honesty of conversations. Can one call during working hours and, if so, what are acceptable topics? Can it be to say "I love you," or only when the keys are locked in the car? Do you assume that evenings will be spent together with the possibility of making other arrangements, or do you come home when you run out of other things to do? Do you have breakfast together? Dinner together? What about praying together? What role do the TV, newspaper, needlepoint, sex, crossword puzzle, computer, friends, sports, telephone, family members, or even sleep play in your home? Having and holding another person means being together in a way that makes sense—that will work for the rest of your life—that is mutually satisfying and allows growth and change.

There is no one way or best way to fulfill this vow. All of us have to learn together and, in the process, each of us must compromise a few assumptions. Patterns for family life are basically learned in the place where we grew up. Those in two-parent homes will begin by either imitating or purposefully avoiding the behavior of their parents. An increasing number of adults have grown up in single-parent homes and have no such example to draw upon. They end up transposing significant relationships between their parent and other family members such as grandparents and siblings, or they use information gleaned from television and neighbors. We have to make the best with what we have been given. At least two things are common to us all no matter where we learned about life sharing. The first is that whatever you knew before will have to be modified because no two couples make the same chemistry. The second is that finding the chemistry that works for your relationship requires some experimentation. In other words, give yourself the freedom to be wrong and the opportunity to improve on your assumptions.

The importance of finding the chemistry, the shared priorities, the life patterns of a relationship, is central. One of the differences between dating and being married is moving the relationship from a series of events to a routine. Learning to love one another deeply, powerfully, and even passionately in the routines of a shared life is one of the great mysteries, and even greater joys, of life. (See Principle Eight: Living together is not a particularly good preparation for marriage.)

## 8. For better or for worse:

This vow and its companions, "for richer for poorer, in sickness and in health," are the promises that nothing is going to happen that will make us break these vows. On the face of it such a pledge seems absurd. No one knows what is going to happen. We are all equally subject to the uncertainties of illness, accident, foolishness, misfortune, and basic perversity. And we all have a breaking point. But this vow is a source of enormous strength in a marriage. It is proclaiming that we are in this together—and, to the end. We will not get up each morning and decide whether or not to remain together. We will rise knowing that whatever this day brings, it will be upon us both. It is brave talk, but history knows well that brave talk helps to make brave people. Marriage works best in the care of people bold in their assumptions about the power of their commitment. The unqualified boldness of the promise helps to sustain the couple through the stresses, messes, and tragedies of life.

There is also a warning about an odd little trap in this vow. When we consider the promise we understandably focus on the negative. We are aware of the dangers of the "worse." What we often do not realize is the danger inherent in "better." That subtle danger enters in the gap between two basic truths about the marriage relationship. The first is that marriage works on the principle of self-giving: People who are consciously trying to give themselves to one another forge a bond that is well-nigh unbreakable, as well as wonderfully rewarding. The second is that it takes effort to be self-giving. Our natural instinct is to be self-serving. During bad times people usually respond with generosity, or at least there is an impulse to do so. We try, or want to try, to offer something of ourselves to help solve the problem. Times of illness, pain, earthquake, fire, and flood tend to call out the best in us, and we are reminded to be self-giving. On the other hand, times of prosperity do not similarly inspire us. When you are OK and I am OK we have no reminder about doing the work of self-giving. We can easily begin to take the other person for granted, to assume that he or she does not need what we have to offer, to pursue our own satisfactions and leave our spouse to do the same. When people are busy, content, and moving along on their own track, the relationship can suffer simply because no one remembers to do the work it requires. Dangerous signs begin to appear. Talk is not about anything shared and becomes shallow, inquiries are divorced from genuine interest, help is not asked for or offered, life is lived in tandem, simultaneously, rather than together. People begin moving toward that popular epitaph for marriages: "We just grew apart."

The response to the danger of "better" is not to court "worse." We could hardly recommend living on the brink of disaster in order to keep up the energy marriage requires. Marriages can avoid the dangers of prosperity by having goals. A goal functions like a chosen adversity. It might be as simple as fixing up the attic or as grand as building a house; it could be learning Swahili or constructing a bridge. Raising children (if it is a shared work) serves nicely. The point is not what kind of goals a marriage needs, but that having goals does help remind people of their need for each other. Marriage goals are different from personal ones. Marriages have goals that make claims upon and promise rewards to both the husband and the wife. It is not the way one helps another, though that is important (see Vow #3, Comfort). It is what makes marriage a common venture. It is a sad commentary on us that we have to be reminded to do the work of being married, but we do. The best of us forget and face the danger of allowing this most precious gift to fall into ruin.

Almost everyone knows to keep an eye out for the "worst" of life. The wise ones know to be aware of the danger of "better," too.

## 9. To cherish:

This is a promise to be a little irrational about each other and the relationship. All the other vows are logical and reasonable. Every relationship from office mate to in-law should have the essence of those vows to some degree. Any friendship or cooperative endeavor relies on commitment, mutual support, the keeping of promises, and so on to make them work. The marriage vows are these common courtesies and general expectations carried to a much higher plane and allowed to work at a much greater intensity, but they are basically the same vows.

"Cherish" is the exception. Ordinary relationships do not require cherishing to make them work. To cherish is, literally, to give more value to something than it obviously has. A cherished memento might be priceless to the owner but only bring five dollars in a flea market. Such cherishing is not logical or reasonable but functions well beyond those categories with an importance that passes understanding. Marriages need to make sense in the way they work. But no marriage can be fulfilled if it is confined to logic. The promise to cherish one another is an agreement to share a life that goes well beyond the confines of reason.

To be cherished is to be given special value. It is to step out of the chorus line of life and into someone's spotlight. It is to be important in ways that can only be expressed in symbols. To be cherished is to be loved romantically, surprisingly, humorously, and deeply. Cherish is where the passion of the initial discovery of one another continues to dwell. It is an essential ingredient in good sex and shared quiet. Cherish provides a limiting boundary for arguments and is what feels good when people make up. It is the engine for gentleness, patience, forgiveness, and understanding. It is the rush of youth, the mortar of all that the marriage builds, and the essence of grief when it is over. Cherish is what passion and peace, concern and courtesy, love and laughter, hope and holiness have in common. Cherish involves feeling, risk, vulnerability, and need. It is the immune system of a marriage. Couples without it are in danger of overreacting to every difficulty that occurs. People who share a sense of being cherished can handle almost anything that comes up between them.

Cherishing can slip out of a marriage without fanfare. People often do not notice that it is missing until a routine misunderstanding slides into a crises or a vague sense of unease refuses to leave the house. The reasons for its loss may be complex or simple. Such circumstances are beyond the scope of this book. But this writer can confirm that what has been lost can be found by people committed to finding it. It may take a little help from each other, a counselor, or a friend. But it can be done.

**10. Until we are parted by death:**

In this promise the couple is affirming that divorce will not be the way they solve their problems. (The question of how else they might handle their differences is addressed in the next section of this book, "The Art of Disagreeing.") Many people think this is the only vow they make in marriage, that the only difference between being married and any other relationship is the fact that it is for life. It is true that lifelong commitment is an essential part of marriage, but the preceding nine promises are really more important than this one. People who pay attention to the first nine rarely have to worry about the tenth one. If all people know about being married is the avoidance of separation, either divorce or a life of unhappiness is likely to be their lot. The nature of marriage is positive, and its health comes from what people actually do for, with, and because of one another. "Not divorced" fails to even come close to describing what it means to be married.

This promise does, however, introduce a significant point about all marriage vows. "Until we are parted by death" is the only qualified statement in the marriage rite. It reminds us that all of the other vows are absolute and not dependent on anything. One does not promise to honor *if* the partner will be honorable. The promise is that I will honor you no matter how you behave, as I will comfort you whether you comfort me or not, and will keep my side of our bargains even if you slip in yours. People often say that marriage is a 50/50 proposition, meaning that both partners must do their part. That is true. But the actual equation is a 100/100 proposition. Healthy and productive marriages require each to give all—not just half—of what appears to be needed. The sentiment that "I will do as much for this marriage as you do" is a deadly one. The marriage needs *all* that *each* of us can do. There is only one qualified phrase among the marriage vows: "Until we are parted by death." Your lawyer will probably tell you that is not much of a loophole. The marriage promises are meant for life, and for good, in both senses of both words. It is meant to last for life and to be for the fulfillment of life. It is for good in that it is final and meant to make our lives better.

## *Beginning to talk about marriage vows:*

Is love a choice or a feeling?

How can your partner help you to have a full life?

What is the "glue" of your relationship? What holds your relationship together?

Do you pray for each other? If so, what is the content of those prayers?

How hard would it be to pray together for each other?

What do you want and need from your partner? What is the difference between what you want and what you need?

Why do you want to be in this relationship?

# PRINCIPLE FIVE

# Marriage vows assume mental health.

## Points of View

A. I don't want to talk about it…It happens all of the time…I am sorry. What else can I say?…I just need more time…I can quit any time I want to… I don't need help. You are the one that needs help…Why?…I didn't mean to.

B. We need to talk…Is marriage supposed to be like this? Do other people live this way?…I don't know what is going on…I am frightened, worried…You never used to be like this…Why?…Time doesn't heal anything, it is what we do with the time that matters…This has to change.

## Principle

One of the best descriptions of mental illness I have heard is "normality out of proportion." This means that mental illness is not something that is completely off the charts or the wall. It is not thinking or acting as no one else does, nor is it only the kind of behavior we think of as crazy. It is a matter of degree, of proportion, of balance. It is normal to have fears. We all have them. But if the fear gets out of balance, if it begins to dominate our lives, then we have a problem with what is called paranoia. By the same token it is normal to go through optimistic periods and pessimistic periods in life. If that mood swing gets out of proportion, we are said to be manic-depressive, which is an illness. Any normal part of the human experience, if carried to the extreme, becomes an illness. If the experience of being married gets out of balance; if the marriage vows are carried to an unhealthy extreme; if either partner has the sense that some part of the relationship is out of control, the marriage is not healthy. Commitment is one thing; obsession is another. Keeping up one's side of the agreement is fine, but being compulsive about it is not. The beauty of being cherished can sicken into suffocation, controlling, and manipulation. Disagreements are good. Fights are not.

The marriage vows are absolute (see p. 51 – #10) but they are bounded by mental health. In my struggles to recognize the dim distinction between what is normal and what is on the other side, I find the concept of "balance" to be very helpful. Individual lives and relationships can get out of balance. When they do, it is time to get help. If one partner begins to think that the relationship is losing that essential balance and proportionality of health, it is time for both to get some help. The feeling that one is being trapped by the devotion of the other is a sign that the couple needs consultation just as surely as panic attacks are an indicator that an individual needs help. When the behavior of your partner seems irrational more often than is comfortable, it is time for a counselor. If drugs or alcohol are becoming more important than you want them to be, it is time for some assistance. Even if the sense cannot be described any better than "it seems to be out of whack," call in the experts. Let them help you see what is going on. And, remember: If one person thinks there is a problem in the marriage, then the marriage has a problem that deserves to be taken seriously by both.

Note that I am suggesting outside professional help at this point. There is no shame in turning to clergy, doctors, or mental health professionals. My experience with "Twelve Step" programs, self-help groups based on the model of Alcoholics Anonymous, is very positive. Groups as well as professionals may vary in their effectiveness and it may take a little work to find the right one, but it is worth it. No one expects you to be married alone (see Principle Six). The shame is in needing help and letting your pride keep you from getting it. People are not expected to operate their cars, air conditioners, finances, dental care, education, or religion without help. Where did we get the idea that we should be able to handle something as complex and profound as our marriages without it?

Put another way: Think of your marriage as a child (see Principle Seven). If your child falls and skins his or her knee, you are supposed to fix it. If the child falls and breaks a leg, it would be stupid, to say nothing of criminal, for you to try to fix it. By the same token, if you and your partner have a disagreement, you are supposed to deal with it. But if the relationship is losing its balance, veering toward something out of control and unhealthy, it would be all wrong for you to try to fix it—alone. Get help! It is out there and it can make a great difference.

## *Beginning to talk about balance in a marriage:*

What words describe the way it feels to you to be in this relationship right now?

What do wise people do when they do not know what to do?

What would be different for you if the marriage were balanced and healthy?

Is change possible for people, for marriages?

How have your feelings changed?

What do you think of the saying: "It is easier to act your way into a new way of feeling than it is to feel your way into a new way acting"?

# The community, congregation, and family make vows, too.

## *Points of View*

A. Their marriage was another triumph of hope over experience…It is none of our business how they live their lives…Does everyone but him know what is going on?…She knows, she just does not want to deal with it…"It was good of God to let Mrs. Carlyle marry Mr. Carlyle thereby making two people miserable instead of four."[4]…I wouldn't know how to bring it up.

B. But these are our best friends. We have to say something…You told Bob his golf swing was wrong and that his smoking was not healthy, why not tell him that the way he treats his wife is out of line?…I do not know what to do either, so our problem is not how to save the marriage but just how to find help. That is something we can do…Jan, this is hard for me to say, but I have been concerned about you and Bob. I sense a lot of tension. At

---

[4]Samuel Butler. From a letter dated 21 Nov. 1884 in *Letters between Samuel Butler and Miss E. M. A. Savage 1871-1885* (London: Cape, 1935).

your wedding I promised to be there for you if you needed me. Would you let me know if there is anything I can do that would be helpful?

## *Principle*

Just as a married couple has responsibilities to the community and families in which they live, those communities and families have responsibilities to the couple. These obligations are included in two promises made during the service. The first is part of almost all weddings and has been for centuries; the second is being found in more and more services. In spite of the wide application, most people do not know about their promises.

The first vow in the wedding is made by the congregation rather than the couple. It comes in the context of a statement most people think is a silly question that invites outbursts by pranksters and jilted lovers. The officiant says: "If any of you can show just cause why they may not lawfully be married, speak now; or else for ever hold your peace." This generally introduces a pregnant pause in which the couples' friends struggle to be serious and is followed by a sigh of relief when the moment is passed. The point of the statement is universally missed. The history of the statement is rooted in the need to establish the legality of a marriage prior to proceeding with the vows. That legal question is still important but is usually addressed in the process of counseling or in acquiring a license. In addition to its ancient legal role, the statement binds the congregation in the marriage covenant. It works this way. If people think that the marriage is a mistake and they care for the couple at all, they should tell them so. It is difficult but right to share their concerns whether they are based on vague suspicion or certain evidence. A bad marriage is a terrible place to be, and we should do all we can to keep our loved ones from experiencing such misery. We need to tell them, but it must be when they can still do something about it, while the relationship belongs to them and they can decide its duration. In a few moments after these vows, the relationship will belong to God, not to the couple. We cannot tear down the things that belong to God. Once the vows are made, our suggestion that the marriage is a blunder and that our friends should get out of it are no longer appropriate. In other words, the congregation must speak now or else forever hold their peace. Obviously the best time to share our views with the couple is long before the ceremony reaches this point. We do not expect anyone to speak at that point, but we do expect everyone to "forever hold their peace." People agree to hold their peace if they have doubts. The promise is that family and friends will do nothing to tear this marriage down or make it more difficult. This is the first promise of the congregation, the community, the friends, and the family.

The second promise is more positive. In the Episcopal *Book of Common Prayer* that I know best, the officiant asks the congregation, "Will all of you witnessing these promises do all in your power to uphold these two persons in their marriage?" The response is to be, "We will." The first promise of family and friends is to keep hands off and mouths shut regarding negative feelings about the marriage. The second promise is to provide all of the encouragement, support and good will that they can to make this marriage a success.

Most people have a natural instinct for these promises. We know to keep quiet when we think someone's spouse is a jerk or a fool. We at least try to be affirming when speaking of another's household. The vows help to remind us that the family and friends of the couple have agreed to a very specific role in this marriage. We are the cheering section and we are available for support. Encouragement has a thousand doors. Support has but one, which can only be opened from the inside. Sometimes it is necessary to knock on that door and ask if the couple will open it to you. Such an inquiry should not be taken lightly but lovingly and sparingly. It is possible to be embarrassingly wrong when we enter uninvited into another's marriage. But, as a friend of mine is fond of saying, "Some things are worth doing badly." You know your friends and family better than I do. Some people need a nudge to get the help they need.

## *Beginning to talk about family and friends' responsibility:*

How do people indicate that they are open or closed to conversations about their personal life?

How do you think your marriage looks to others?

How would you want someone to "knock at the door of your marriage" to ask if you need help?

What is it that makes talking to others, even professionals, about our marriage so difficult?

How can people be supportive of other people's marriages?

Whom do you trust enough to ask for help or insight into your marriage?

What is the worst thing that can happen?

If you are reading this book because your marriage is in pain, I imagine that you are getting pretty fed up with the positive nature of what is being said so far. Your sense may be these things are not possible for you, the ideas are not working in your relationship, the vulnerability required to participate in these promises is too dangerous, or that the ideal 100/100 equation for healthy households is way out of balance in your experience. This book may help you to identify what is missing or what needs to be brought into balance. It can help to start or redirect a conversation that you and your partner need to have. If that is not workable or possible, remember the second vow of the community: We will do all that we can to uphold you in your marriage. That promise is binding not only on those present but upon all of us. The point is that you do not have to be married alone. You do not have to solve every problem that comes up. Some of them are too big. Some are too emotional for you or your spouse to think about clearly. Some are just beyond your experience, but not necessarily beyond the experience of others. Get help!

The community promised to help, but they also promised not to butt in. People will not help unless you ask. If the pain is too great, the problem too big, call a professional, call someone you trust, call someone you respect, call the people you need. Marriage is no bed of roses. But it is not meant to be a bed of thorns, either. There is no disgrace in asking for help. The only disgrace is in pretending that you are dealing with important issues when you are not. Such fantasies are unworthy of the reasons for your life.

And remember: If one of you thinks there is a problem with the marriage, then both of you have a problem. If your spouse thinks the marriage needs help, it probably does. Get help!

## PRINCIPLE SEVEN

# Divorce is a reality
# and a possibility.

## *Points of View*

A. Don't we owe it to ourselves to know why we are having trouble? We talked a lot about why we wanted to get married, why can't we talk about why we are separating?...Love is choosing. Why are we not choosing each other? What are we choosing instead?...I said I am sorry. What more do you want?...She means nothing to me...We haven't tried to work it out...You are overreacting.

B. We have the same argument over and over... Maybe I am not cut out for marriage...I just do not love you anymore...I cannot live like this anymore...I do not know what it is. I just want out...I just cannot get him out of my mind...Nothing ever changes...I have to see if that is what I need to do...I need to be: on my own; by myself; free; alone; away from here; back home; young again...When will you grow up?...When will you get off my back?...Overreacting is the only way I can get your attention.

# *Principle*

In the District of Columbia where I live, the city government is rarely praised for its subtlety in the use of symbolism. One place where such praise might be given (if one believed it was done on purpose) is the location of the marriage license bureau. The happy couple walks past these doors on the way to pick up their license: Domestic Violence Center, Probation Intake, Child Support Enforcement, Child Neglect & Abuse, Mental Retardation & Mental Health. Most couples breeze by without noticing, but the message is there for the keen-eyed. Things can go wrong in life, even when they begin with the highest of hopes. Every divorce has some kind of joyful expectation in its background.

Divorce is becoming so much a part of our common life that some have suggested we change our standard from monogamy to sequential monogamy. In other words, we should no longer expect people to be married to just one person, but to one person at a time. Young people interviewed by the National Marriage Project at Rutgers University indicated that few expect to be wed for life (64% in 1995 as opposed to 68% in 1976) and that only 30% figured that they would be happier married than not married.[5] It may be obvious to the reader by now that this is not the assumption of this writer. The commitment here is to take seriously the ways that a marriage can last a lifetime. In spite of that commitment, one has to acknowledge the reality of divorce. No modern book on marriage can be complete without it.

----

[5]Daniel S. Levy, "Your Family," *Time Magazine,* July 12, 1999.

I understand divorce in this way: When people get married the marriage is like a child of theirs. It is a projection of both of them but it is not either one of them. The marriage is part of each of them but it is something separate from them as individuals. It is never "my marriage"; it is always "our marriage." Like a child the marriage needs to be nurtured and allowed to mature. No marriage on its tenth anniversary (birthday) should be just as it was on its first anniversary. Marriages should grow wiser and deeper with experience as some thorny issues are behind and new ones emerge. Marriages, like children, need to be educated. Couples can learn more about how to deal with one another, respond to one another, and love one another. They can learn about one another's strengths and weaknesses. People can learn how to approach difficult topics and when to be serious. Like children, marriages need to be played with and enjoyed. Fun is, thankfully, a central part of the business of both growing up and being married.

It is also true that both marriages and children sometimes get sick or hurt and have to be cared for. There are the routine bruises of life—the insensitive word, the flared anger, the bad day, the tense moment. And there are major crises—recurring confrontations, unbridgeable gaps in assumptions, clashes of priority, grievous errors. During these times some response is necessary. Children cannot be ignored when they are in pain and neither can relationships. Smaller issues can be dealt with at home. Conversation coupled with forgiveness, understanding, sensitivity, appreciation, and affection usually do the trick. It is hard to talk when one would rather not and even harder to listen when what is being said is embarrassing or painful. Conversation is not always pleasant, but it is necessary and the consequences of not addressing those routine pains is enormous. Sometimes the issue is greater than the couple can handle by themselves. In the same way that the parents of a child are not expected to set a broken leg or remove an appendix, neither is a couple expected to handle every issue of marriage at home. There are times when professional help is needed. There is no shame in needing help, only in not asking for it when it is needed. During such crises the marriage, like a sick child, may need extra time or money. Like anxious parents, an anxious couple need extra support from one another as well as from others who may know about the situation. When a marriage or a child is sick, priorities need to be rearranged and resources redirected. Extraordinary efforts are called for.

But when a child, or a marriage, dies it needs to be buried. Divorce is a funeral for a dead marriage. As at any funeral people need to grieve about what was and what might have been. People in grief need to ask "why," whether they can answer it or not. They need to be angry at themselves and, perhaps, others. People with dead marriages, like those with dead children, have important and significant work to do before life can return to its proper track. Anne Morrow Lindbergh wrote these words to her mother after the tragic kidnapping and murder of her son: "I do not believe that sheer suffering teaches. If suffering alone taught, all the world would be wise, since everyone suffers. To suffering must be added mourning, understanding, patience, love, openness, and the willingness to remain vulnerable."[6] Divorced people have the same work to do.

Divorce can only be understood in the context of the lifelong nature of a marriage. Divorce is not a problem-solving technique nor the antidote to boredom nor an excuse to avoid the issues of life. One of the particular misfortunes of our age is that people come too quickly to the decision to give up on a marriage. The Rutgers study cited above concluded that the growing economic independence of women and the rising number of children of divorce help to make divorce more of an option. It is possible to think that some are inadvertently programmed for divorce by the models given in their families and society at large. When coupled with those who are simply unprepared for sustaining relationships, one can see that our defenses against divorce are getting thinner. For many with these backgrounds it seems that divorce is preferable to a serious conversation; a life apart is chosen over a moment of truth. Marriage can be hard and uncomfortable. I cannot think of anything really worthwhile that does not have that possibility. But what is difficult is not the same as what is hopeless. Divorce is what needs to be done when what was supposed to live is found to be dead. Divorcing too soon is like burying a sick child. Divorcing too late is like living with an open casket in the house. Divorce, when it is right, is the most loving thing that a couple can do for one another. Divorce is something that has to happen when everything— absolutely everything—has been tried. When the relationship reaches a toxic level that makes it impossible, it is time to end it. Divorce does not kill marriage. Divorce is a funeral for a relationship that has been killed by something else.

---

[6]Anne Morrow Lindbergh, *Hour of Gold, Hour of Lead— Diaries of Anne Morrow Lindbergh, 1929-1932* (New York: Harcourt, Brace, Jovanovich, 1973), p. 214.

One reason divorce is so prevalent among us is that it has an advantage over marriage. Marriage takes the cooperation of two people. A divorce can be summoned by only one. If one person simply stops being married, stops doing the work of maintaining and nurturing the relationship, the marriage will die. It may be kept on life support by one person's energy or by the desire to appear happy, or it may hang on as something just above a coma with minimal signs of life for a period of time. But when one person stops being married, the marriage stops living and begins to die. It is painful, unfortunate, frustrating, and terribly sad. But it is true. In my experience many people opt out of marriage simply because they do not know how to do the work it requires. If people, male or female, are not taught how to identify and express sensitivity, they are ill-equipped for the work of marriage. People who do not know how to disagree well, those whose choices are limited to denying the reality of conflict or lashing out destructively, are not likely to be successful in developing deep and satisfying relationships. A good disagreement will leave a couple closer at its finish than they were before it began (see Principles Eleven through Fifteen). People who love one another can teach and learn how to do that work. Those who continually learn from one another know that it is the most joyful and rewarding work in life, even though it still can be hard work. Those who have not and will not acquire the thought and communication skills that lifelong, continually deepening, mutually fulfilling relationships need, are like witch doctors in an epidemic. They apply primitive formulas, perhaps with conviction and energy, but without any real effect on the problem. Many marriages end unnecessarily in the care of such practitioners.

Marriages die for any of a number of reasons. Each divorce, like each marriage, has some things in common with all other divorces and some things that make this one unique. Any autopsy for the deceased relationship should be done by professionals, not by family and friends. Divorced persons need the support and help of those closest to them as they do the hard work of moving from suffering to "the willingness to remain vulnerable." Suggestions about what went wrong, taking sides, admitting that you thought it was a mistake from the beginning, or any other form of intervention—unless specifically requested by the divorced person—are not very helpful. A simple truth about life is that it only goes in one direction, and that is forward. While there is hope, we all have a commitment to join in the fight to save the marriage. After the funeral/divorce people need to weep, be angry, forgive, become wiser, and then join in the inevitable flow of life toward the future. The past has to be left where it was buried.

## *Beginning to talk about divorce:*

What do you think people should do before talking about a divorce?

Have our backgrounds prepared us to make our marriage work, or have we been programmed for divorce?

Did people in your family avoid conflicts, or did they deal with them and resolve issues? How did they do that, and what can we learn from that example?

What do our problems have to teach us about ourselves and our marriage?

Why did we get married in the first place? What has happened to those reasons? Do they still have any power?

Can we choose to be vulnerable to one another again?

Whom do we know who can help us? (If you draw a blank on this one, call a church and ask them to recommend a reputable marriage counselor. If that church cannot or will not, call another church.)

## PRINCIPLE EIGHT

# Living together is not a particularly good preparation for marriage.

### Points of View

**A.** Think of the money we would save…We could see if we want to get married…Who cares what people think? This is just about us…I love you and I want to be with you…Most of my clothes are over at your place anyway…I am not ready to get married right now…Everybody does it…Wouldn't it be better to be together?…This way, if we get married we will already know everything we need to know about living together.

**B.** If we are ready to live together, why aren't we ready to get married? What is the difference?…What is the future we are working toward?…How would this end? How would it move forward?…I don't want a day-to-day relationship with you…What about children?…I love you and I want to share a commitment with you…I don't know if I am ready to spend all of my time with you.

## Principle

I do not perform many weddings these days for couples who have not been living together prior to the ceremony. It may be a reality limited to my location or experience, but I do not think so. I believe it is a growing practice. And why not? I have been told by couples that the arrangement is cheaper and that sharing an apartment allows them to start marriage on a firmer financial footing. There is no doubt about that. Others point out that it is a way to get to know one another in the routine of life, which I often say is the real arena of married life. I cannot deny it. It can readily be pointed out that sleeping together has become accepted, and apparently expected, in even the shallowest of relationships. The old sin of fornication, which means sexual intercourse by unmarried people, seems to be defenseless in the face of a swarm of movies, ads, and assumptions about sex. Certainly there is very little, if any, social pressure for abstinence. And even though no one ever tells me it is a reason for moving in with one another, I know it is fun to play house with someone you are fond of.

These are obvious benefits to premarital housekeeping. But there are at least two real dangers in it that few people seem to take into account. Living together fools people into thinking they are experimenting with marriage when it is impossible to do so. And living together weakens the basis for the decision to be married.

It fools people in this way. Marriage is a lifelong commitment. Living together may look like a "trial marriage," but there is no such thing as a trial lifelong commitment. Being in a relationship where the commitment is defined and informed, as in marriage, is very different from trying something out. The bond and the joy of marriage are part of one another. People who live together certainly have a commitment to one another, but unless it is of the "until we are parted by death" kind, it is not much like marriage. Walking around with your eyes closed is not the same as being blind. Being a good student is not the same as being a scholar. Making money is not the same as being a breadwinner for a family. Playing a lot of golf is not much like being on the pro tour. High school is not the same as college. Virtual realty is not reality. A video game is not combat even though it may simulate it in many regards. Being an assistant is not the same as being in charge. Knowing your parents will bail you out is not the same as being on your own no matter how far you go. By the same token, living together is not the same thing as marriage (see Principle Two for more on Commitment).

Obviously people can learn about marriage by living together. But only a little bit. No one can argue that the increase in the numbers of people who live together before marriage has introduced any noticeable decline in the divorce rate. The commitment of marriage provides a security, a safety net, a protective ring around a relationship. The strength of the commitment allows people the freedom to experiment, to make mistakes and to learn. These are the basic tools required for growth in life's major enterprises, including marriage. The freedom for such growth is in direct proportion to the strength of the commitment in the relationship. Living together generally lacks the maximum level of commitment that is basic to marriage. Cohabiting may be a "trial marriage" but to be a "trial" it must exclude the deep commitment that is at the heart of the marriage covenant. "Trial marriage" is an oxymoron, a contradiction in terms like "jumbo shrimp." A shared life thrives on a continual sense of exploration, discovery, adventure, and vitality. The lifelong commitment of marriage provides an undergirding for those exercises that living together cannot.

There is another difference between the commitment to share life and the decision to share a dwelling. Living together, because it is an agreement between two people, does not have the strength of a public marriage, which is an agreement involving the couple, their families, their community, and their God. It is like the difference between a decision to diet or quit smoking that is made privately rather than publicly. The glue of that public commitment is greater and we stick to it better. This factor will vary in its influence from couple to couple, but it does make a difference.

That tired old sin, fornication, is worth a second look at this point. As indicated above, it means sexual intercourse by unmarried persons and it is regarded as wrong. The reason for this is not another case of old people trying to take away the fun of young people. Like most prohibitions against sin, it is designed to keep people from getting hurt. In this case it grows out of respect for the binding power of sexual intercourse. People who know one another sexually have a bond between them that is powerful and unlike that which comes from other shared experiences. That binding power is the reason ancient temples often included prostitutes. The sexual act represented the bond between the believer and the god. The Judeo-Christian prohibition against fornication is saying that people should not be bound together more closely than they intend. Sexual intercourse is for permanent relationships, not ones that are likely to be temporary. The end of a relationship that has such a bond is too painful. It hurts the people involved or, what is worse, it allows or requires people to deny the bonding power of making love. When that power is denied, sex becomes a casual thing, and a wonderful gift from God is abused and diminished. Casual sex comes with a high price tag. The cost is taken from the power of a sexual relationship to forge a unique and intimate bond between two people. That is why fornication is held to be a mistake.

In the context of the decision to live together, fornication can trick people into thinking that the sexual bond is enough to hold the marriage together. More than one couple have confused good sex with a good relationship. Living together and sleeping together introduce a powerful force into a delicate period of growth, understanding, and decision-making. Sharing a home is fun, economical, educational, and generally acceptable. But for unmarried couples it does tend to confuse the questions that need to be considered on the way to the altar.

The other danger in living together is what it does to the marriage decision-making process. The decision to marry is a hard one. It does not come from adding pluses and subtracting minuses. It is highly subjective and is not preceded by a "therefore." Marriage must be thought through carefully and approached with caution. It is something done with the head at the urging of the heart. Passion may raise the question of marriage, but the best answers come from the intellect. The fires of love will last longer and burn brighter in a well-chosen spot where new fuel is available and the wind is steady. Marriage is choosing the person who will be the biggest influence in your life. It involves the families of which your new family is a part. It involves the community and, in many cases, the church. It is not a private decision at all, but is a public venture onto holy ground. The decision to live together is rarely any of these things. It is not made lightly, but it does not have the complex framework of the decision to marry. If things don't go well, one can always move out. It is your life, your decision. No one else need be involved.

Once people are living together the basis for the decision to marry changes. Instead of the demanding question, "Why should I marry this person?", it becomes "Why not marry this person?" The latter is an easier question that is less likely to produce a satisfactory life-long answer. The burden of proof, to use a legal term, shifts. Since we are here together and things seem to be going well, no real problems to speak of, why not go ahead and get married? If we do not get married, what will we do? Break up? There is not enough friction for that? Just keep living together for all of our lives or until one of us gets a better offer? Most people want a more stable basis for home life than that. So why not get married? It is a weak line of reasoning for a marriage. It operates on the absence of negatives rather than the presence of positives. The decision to marry should be a clear positive act of choosing the person who will be the greatest influence in your life. It wants to be the conscious choice of a public commitment to one another, the larger family and community, and God. It should not be just the next step after deciding first to sleep together, then to live together.

Obviously I have no idea what is in the mind of every person who decides to turn living together into matrimony. The line of reasoning outlined above includes many points I have heard couples make as they approach marriage. Some of those marriages have worked out wonderfully well. Some have not. The success or failure of a marriage involves many more issues than just whether people lived together before the ceremony. A survey taken in England in the early 1990s indicated that people who live together before marriage have a slightly higher incidence of divorce than those who do not. *The Washington Post* reported, "In Australia cohabiting is statistically considered one of the three premarital experiences contributing most to the risk of divorce. The other two are having a child out of wedlock and leaving home at an early age."[7] My suggestion is that cohabiting before marriage tricks people into thinking they know what marriage really is and makes the decision to be married more difficult.

---

[7] Barbara Mathias-Riegel, "The Altered State of Matrimony," *The Washington Post*, 8 October 1998, D4.

### *Beginning to talk about living together:*

Do you believe those things about fornication and the binding power of sexual intercourse?

What is living together a step toward? What, if anything, does it say about our future?

Under what conditions would we stop living together?

What do you know about other couples who have lived together? Did it help them or hurt them? How?

What promises are we making to each other if we decide to move in together?

# PRINCIPLE NINE

# Sex and money are symbols.

## Points of View

**A.** We are getting in over our heads…We have to save for a rainy day…We need to take small steps. We cannot do everything now…We cannot expect to live the way our parents do after they have spent long years working and saving…Credit cards are killing us…We cannot live on borrowed money…People get rich slowly. Your schemes are too quick and they never work…You think you are having a brainstorm when you are really just partly cloudy…How can you think about sex at a time like this?…Can't we just be close without the groping?…I don't care how Debbie did Dallas. I do not want to do that…"Now after loving me late at night…you just roll over and turn out the light."[8]

**B.** Life is meant to be enjoyed…We can pay it off… Something will come along, it always does…But we need this…I thought you would like it…I cannot go to the theater looking like this…We have to dress for success…I do not have time to look everywhere for a

---

[8]Neil Diamond and Alan and Marilyn Bergman, "You Don't Bring Me Flowers Anymore" lyrics (1991).

better buy. I would rather spend my time making money...Of course labels matter, that is why they put them in clothes...Sex is supposed to be fun...Come on, loosen up a little...You cannot be that tired all of the time...We do the same thing every time...You get your satisfaction but you forget about mine..."When it's good for you, babe, and you're feeling all right."[9]

## *Principle*

Almost everyone who writes about marriage is obliged to include something about sex and money. The common attitude seems to be that they hold the key to success or misery in a relationship. There is no denying that they are important, but our culture gives them far more attention than they deserve. It is true that every marriage has to deal with them. Some people seem to be really good at either one or the other and, I suppose, some are gifted in both. There are many who cannot seem to handle either one. Both sex and money have the power to mess up people's heads by acquiring more importance than is healthy. The world is full of experts on both subjects, and those who need help should be able to find it. My wish for people is that they have plenty of both sex and money, and enjoy them generously, wisely, and with a sense of humor.

In spite of all of the media and conversational attention given to sex and money, very little is said about the symbolic role they play in our lives. When we understand them as symbols, it is easier to have a helpful conversation

---

[9]Neil Diamond and Alan and Marilyn Bergman, "You Don't Bring Me Flowers Anymore" lyrics (1991).

about them. A symbol points beyond itself to something greater. A flag is just cloth but it represents a whole nation, its history, people, and potential. A designer's label is meant to indicate a lifestyle. A uniform proclaims a role backed by an institution. A Star of David or a cross point beyond themselves to a belief and beyond that to the realities behind those beliefs. The meaning of symbols is not fixed but varies depending on who is observing it. Flags have moved people to kill or to serve depending on how they related to the symbol. Advertisers go to incredible lengths to get us to associate positive thoughts with product logos. Uniforms and religious symbols have a long bloody history of differing interpretations.

When we think of money as symbol we can recognize that it has little real value in and of itself. Most of what passes for money these days are just numbers on paper. Few of us actually give or receive anything of real value when we buy or sell. Instead we transmit green paper, a signed promissory note, or electronic blips stimulated by a plastic card. Our salaries are usually a notice that the numbers associated with our name at the bank have been changed to higher numbers. The value of these transactions is symbolic because they only have the meaning we agree that they have. And we have agreed that they have great value.

Money is the way our society assigns worth. To ascribe worth is the literal meaning of "worship" so symbolically money is the same as a prayer or a hymn. Each expresses what we most value in life. For this reason we feel undervalued by a low salary, take pride in objects that required large sums to get, worry over whether something we want is "worth it," and gloat when we find a bargain. This process of using money to assign worth takes us to the heart of the matter, which is the question of priorities. Will we spend money on drapes or a TV? Do we give priority to playing lotto or supporting a charity? Which are the necessities of life and which are the niceties? Should we allocate our funds to clothes or tickets to the game, a nice car or furniture, alcohol or the Internet? Money gives expression to our sense of security, confidence, success, and pride. All of these are important in life but none has a fixed monetary value. Nor do they have a place in our minds. Most of our attitudes toward these things were shaped in childhood and are not beyond reexamining or realigning in adulthood. Couples with a conflicting sense of what life is about and the importance of success and security will often discover those differences while dealing with money because it is the primary symbol we have for value and priority. The important thing to know is that discussions about money are not often about cash. They are about the priorities and values.

Sex has a similar role in a relationship. Indeed, the 1992 National Health and Social Life Survey, the most comprehensive look at American sexual experience since the Kinsey Reports, finds a direct corollary between economic stress and sexual satisfaction.[10] Sexual relationships are, in my opinion, more complex than financial ones. They are affected by biology (sexual needs differ), psychology (marriage takes some of the edge off of sex as seduction and conquest) and even chronology (morning people often marry night people). In addition, health problems impact sexual experience as do traumas like sexual abuse. I cannot

---

[10]John Schwartz, "Study Uncovers High Rates of Bedroom Blues," *The Washington Post*, 10 February 1999, A1.

pretend to know how to unravel its mysteries, but I can say some things that are true that may be helpful.

Like money, the meaning of sex is not confined to itself. G. K. Chesterton's assertion that in sex "the pleasure is momentary, the position is absurd, and the expense is enormous" is wonderfully clever but a little harsh because it confines its understanding to the sexual act itself. But clearly there is more to sex than the simple act of intercourse. For one thing, conjugal sex has a way of mirroring the whole relationship, and in that way symbolizes it. A sexual relationship is different from a sexual act because it has no clear beginning and end. It combines all that goes on at breakfast and in the living room. Those who have discovered the personal pleasure of giving satisfaction to another can find opportunities for joy in every room of the house. A couple that is distant and hostile during the day is not likely to be loving and embracing at night. Exploitive, manipulative, and demanding verbal relationships make spontaneous, generous, and satisfying sexual relationships very difficult. A marriage that is beginning to weaken and fray will often show its first signs of stress in the way people make love. The sense that something is missing in the bedroom is usually an indication that something is actually missing in the living room. It is hard to talk about sex with someone we have sex with. It may be comforting to know that most of the conversations about sex actually should be conversations about the way we talk to one another. There are sexual problems deeply rooted in psychology and physiology that require expert intervention. I would not suggest, however, that a couple concerned about their sexual relationship begin with sex therapy. The place to begin is with what they already know best: how they feel about being in this relationship, and what is their experience of being honored, cherished, taken seriously, and enjoyed by their partner. Most of what is wrong—and good—about sex can be found there.

Our culture teaches us that sex and money are able to make sense out of life. Books, magazines, advertisements, movies, and television all assure us over and over that a relationship with lots of money and good sex will meet our needs. Enormous sums, vast energy, and countless hours are spent in following that dream. Modern snake oil salesmen and women insist that just looking sexy and appearing prosperous will be fulfilling. Unfortunately the meaning of life is seldom found on the surface. The car we drive, the jewelry we wear, where we buy clothes, or who we manage to have sex with is not going to get close to the heart of any matter of real consequence. The fact is that life makes sense out of sex—not the other way around. There is no amount of money that can give meaning to anyone's life. It is the meaning of our lives that gives value to money. (Read those last three sentences over again slowly until you have them clearly fixed in your mind.)

### *Beginning to talk about money and sex:*

What were the attitudes toward money in the home in which you were raised?

Do you still agree with what you learned then?

What was your first experience with your own money?

How would you describe yourself in relation to money? How would you describe your partner?

In your ideal budget, what percentage would you allot to savings, charity, entertainment, things for your home?

Can you do that now?

What does it feel like to be in this relationship right now?

Have your feelings changed? How?

Debra Haffner of the Education Council of the United States says Americans are "mildly erotophobic," which means afraid of sexuality and unwilling to discuss it. Do you agree? What might make it hard to for a person to discuss a sexual relationship?

Has your sexual relationship changed? If so, is it better or worse? Why?

# PRINCIPLE TEN

# Children are hard on marriage.

## Points of View

A. My biological clock is ticking…It will be good for us, bring us closer together…Your parents keep asking when they will be grandparents…I don't know why, but I just get weepy when I see baby things…Brian and Jane are expecting a baby; so are the Thompsons… Nobody can actually afford to have children. You just have them and it works out…Families with a lot less money have children and they seem OK…*and later…*We have to for the sake of the children…I just want to sleep… The doctor said…Jeremy did the cutest thing today…We have to start thinking about college expenses…Shh, the children will hear us.

B. We can't afford children…I am not ready for the responsibility…How can we have children when we haven't even paid off our own student loans?…Why should I give up my career to stay at home? Why don't you give up yours?…Aren't we happy the way we are?… I do not want a kid who behaves the way I did growing up…But we are already a family…Why don't we just offer to baby sit for Brian and Jane?…*and later…*I can't right now, honey, I have to work…One more word out of

Barney and I am shooting the TV set…I'm too tired right now, maybe later…These kids are driving me crazy…Turn that damn thing down!

## *Principle*

Being a parent is probably the most important, creative, frustrating, rewarding, stimulating, draining, exciting, irritating, challenging, and meaningful enterprise in the human experience. Volumes have been written on the subject and no doubt many more will be. This book, however, is about marriage, not parenting. Our focus is on the two people who are at the center of every family, not the numbers of children in orbit around them. It is important to know the difference. Marriage is about two people. Parenting, ideally, involves three or more. Marriage is something adults do as peers. Children are not adults, and their relationship with parents is not one of equality. In spite of these obvious differences, one of the easiest mistakes made by couples is confusing parenting with marriage. Because a day at the park with the children is such a good thing for everyone, including the parents, it is often allowed to substitute for an adult evening out. They are both healthy, fun, and necessary but they are not the same thing. B and C are both vitamins people need but they cannot be substituted for one another. The needs and wonder of children are so compelling, their presence so demanding, their rights so clear, and their potential so limitless that they can take over a marriage without anyone noticing it. It is easy to let the affairs of children become the parents' main topic of conversation and then subtly become their only topic.

The possibility of an emotionally adulterous relationship with a child (see p. 42 – #6) is always present. Shared parenting is a great source of strength to a relationship, but the overlap of parenting and marriage obscures the differences between them. Marriages need more than parenting, just as they need more than good sex and money in the bank, to stay healthy.

Children are hard on a marriage. While giving joy and calling out the best in us, they also make demands, take time, and cause trouble. It is hard to explain to a hungry baby that you really need to talk with one another for awhile. It is difficult for people to agree on common principles of responsibility, discipline, and expectations. Children do not have any responsibility for making the relationship between parents better. A child's concept of the family does not usually include any understanding of a relationship between the parents except as it impacts the life of the child. Children have no idea of the love or difficulties between the mother and the father or of other pressures that might influence home life. Because children do not know of the multiple layers of family relationships, they often experience guilt when the marriage in their family ends in divorce. Small children often agonize over what they have done to end their parent's marriage. Even older children who have an intellectual understanding of marriage relationships do not usually have a profound perception of what is between married adults. One of the great shocks of leaving home is coming back and find-ing out that one's parents have managed to carry on in your absence—which indicates that they do actually have a relationship that does not include you. Since children have no real concept of the marriage, they can be expected to do little or nothing to make it better. The idea that a troubled marriage could be helped by having children is like trying to put out a fire with logs. It normally makes matters worse and increases the consequences of failure.

Raising children takes time. Couples planning a family often wonder whether they can afford to have children. By this they usually mean having enough money. While this is important, it is not as important as the question of being able to afford the time to raise children. Most people I know do not have enough money to have children, but they do it anyway. The money question tends to solve itself as parents willingly shift their priorities to the lives of the children. Time, however, remains a difficult question. It takes time to provide the foundation of love, support, discipline, and values that children need to become strong, healthy, and happy people. New parents are often shocked to discover that the decision to have a child is also a decision to stop doing a number of other things that are important and meaningful. The question of children is also a question of having time to do the things that give meaning to our lives, to earn the money we think we need, and do the work of maintaining our marriage. It can be done, and when it is done life moves to a deeper level of meaning, purpose, and focus that can only be experienced, not imagined.

Another reason children are difficult for marriage has to do with the dynamics of relationships. The growth pattern of the relationship between parents and children is different from that of any other. All of us meet one another in a state of separation and are meant to grow closer. This is true of marriages, friendships, business associations, and neighbors. All relationships have the ideal of growing closer as they continue toward a perfect union. In this they are like an arch (see figure 1). Obviously none ever get to a perfect state, but they all have that as an ideal. The relationship with a child

**Figure 1:**

**All relationships are meant to grow toward a state of perfect union.**

is different. It begins in a state of perfect union in the womb and is meant to grow apart as the child moves from complete dependence to an appropriate independence. When the child is mature, an adult relationship with parents becomes possible and they can begin to move toward a newer, deeper, and closer life together. The parent-child relationship grows in a diamond pattern as the child grows from dependence to independence to interdependence (figure 2). It is difficult for parents to keep their lives growing together while enabling their children to grow away from them. Adults can get confused about the importance of the marriage as an anchor for all other family relationships. Husbands and wives who have very different roles as parents may find the marriage dynamic being pulled apart by the responsibilities of raising children. Parents who allow the intimacy of husband and wife to be replaced by the changing intimacy of parent and child are very close to serious trouble.

Marriages do not need children. They are complete when the couple comes together. Children are a joyful addition meant to pass through the marriage in the diamond pattern mentioned above. But children need marriages. They grow best in a home made loving and safe by the strength of the marriage at its center. The parents need to provide a firm, safe, and supportive arena for the development and maturation of children. Failure to do so is not good for adults or children (figure 3). As a self-guided tour brochure at a tourist site so gently expressed

**Figure 2:**

The exception is parent and child, which begins in a state of perfect union, works toward separation and independence, and then seeks a new adult relationship.

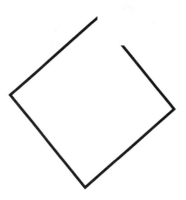

it, "Our observation over the years shows that adults get lost when they let young children lead the way."[11] It is true of homes as well as aircraft carriers. Parents need to be in charge and their authority needs to be rooted in their commitment to one another. Disagreements about something as important as raising children are bound to take place. But nothing can be allowed to shake the foundation which the marriage provides for the whole family. There is an old question and answer which has much wisdom. The question is, "What is the best thing a father can do for his

**Figure 3:**
The dynamic of the parent-child relationship (union to separation and independence) is counter to the dynamic of a marriage (growing toward perfect union).

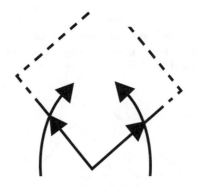

The Point: Kids can be hard on a marriage.

---

[11]USS Yorktown, Patriot's Point, Charleston, S.C.

children?" The answer is, "Love their mother." The point applies to mothers as well.

Marriage takes energy and effort; so does raising children. They are not exactly the same kind of energy or the same sort of effort. The special needs of a marriage can be postponed for just so long before a toll begins to be taken. I have been told that the peak years for divorces are at two, five, and twenty-five years of marriage. While no divorce has a single cause, the factor of children seems crucial at these key points in a couple's history. The second year of marriage is usually not affected by children. It is when people who never should have gotten married in the first place begin to see the error of their decision. The fifth year, however, is when children tend to make their presence felt in the house and begin to make unique demands on the marriage. Twenty-five years is about the time children are leaving the house. Couples who have confused parenting with marriage or put off doing the work of marriage or allowed the kids to be all they talked about find that their reason for being together left with the last child. Such marriages often come apart with a sigh and a bewildered look. Marriages need the sound of two people talking. They need the kind of love that is for adults only. Being together needs to keep its original reasons and find ways to discover new ones. Children cannot help with these things. But those children who are raised in a household where these things are done are fortunate indeed.

## *Beginning to talk about children:*

What do you remember about your own childhood that seems important as we consider having children?

What do we have to offer a child? What would it require of us to give that to a child?

How will we work on our marriage when we have children?

What do I need from you when we are parents?

What can you expect from me when we are parents?

Are there any genetic issues we need to find out about?

What would be the most fun about having children?

# DISAGREEING WELL

# Good disagreements
# make a relationship stronger.

## Points of View

**A.** I can't stand conflict...I just clam up. I refuse to be part of an argument...I can't think of anything to say...I need to sleep on it...Whenever I say anything that upsets you, you start to cry...This is not a court room. Don't try to cross examine me...When you ask me how I feel and I say I don't know, it's because I really don't know...

**B.** We need to talk...I just get things off my chest and then I forget about it...I cannot carry on a conversation by myself...Turn off the TV and talk to me!...Can't I state an opinion without a major blow up?...Just let it all hang out...What comes up comes out...Talking with you is like trying to defuse a bomb...You like the way our bodies are different, why not our minds?

## Principle

Most people who choose to marry do so on the basis of what they have in common. This is certainly understandable and quite important. Our common interests, views, hopes, values, and enthusiasms provide much of the magnetism that draws lovers together. Physical attraction by itself is wonderful, but it cannot sustain a relationship for anywhere near a lifetime. It must be enhanced and reinforced by a sense of commonality that extends through the mental, spiritual, and emotional as well as the physical. Most couples I know trace the development of their relationship through a series of discoveries of mutual interests. A great conversation in which each felt heard and understood is often the turning point between a casual and a serious romance. When asked why couples want to marry, the most frequent responses include "we have so much in common." It is an obvious reason for love and an important one. How could there be a healthy marriage when there is not a healthy balance of shared interests? Indeed, the absence of shared interests is often cited as reason for divorce.

The energy of marriage comes from what people have in common. The art of marriage, however, is in how they handle those things they do not have in common. Learning to disagree well is an essential skill for those who wish to fashion lifelong, life-giving relationships.

Many of us grow up with the notion that disagreements are bad and are to be avoided. Impressionable children are often scolded for arguing. Few parents allow themselves to have a dispute "in front of the children," thereby depriving them of good examples of how people who love one another can disagree. Some adults are so bad at disagreeing that they have no healthy example to share. Their children generally are so appalled by the violence, shouting, door slamming, sulking, and threats of their parents that they vow to spend the rest of their lives in avoidance of all conflict. Others too readily accept such violence as the only realistic response to conflict. These views are held at a terrible price. The fact is that God went to a lot of trouble to make each of us unique. We view events differently, we think in unlike patterns, we are moved by different forces, cadenced by different drummers. Our lists of needs do not often coincide and our wants even more rarely do. We come from different places, our destinations change, our paths diverge. To deny that uniqueness is to deny something of ourselves. If such denial becomes a pattern we begin to be less than we were created to be. It has been wisely said that when two people agree on everything, one of them is not necessary. Being unnecessary because constant agreement is required is belittling. It forces us to deny our deepest views and stay in denial or let the relationship become so shallow that no point made is worth contesting. Such diminishment is frustrating at best, destructive at worst. To affirm our uniqueness is to have conflict. It is as built into the fullness of life as flying is built into birds and discovery into childhood.

Disagreements can harm people and relationships. The story of human life cannot be told apart from this fact. But people can and do learn to disagree well. It is far more common than many would believe. We do not hear much about good arguments because they are not news or gossip worthy. Good disagreements are the bedrock of all human endeavor, especially marriage.

Disagreements are good when people learn from them and use that knowledge to make a better relationship.

Disputes can clarify or provide insight where it had been lacking before. They can be disillusioning when we are disappointed to find that our partner holds a certain view, but in order to be "disillusioned" people have to be "illusioned" in the first place. Marriage is no place for misconceptions and fantasies. It needs and deserves reality. Many of life's realities are discovered in the process of arguing. Such arguments are hard but ultimately good for the relationship.

People can be enriched by their differences. It is possible to recognize and value the uniqueness—even the quirkiness—of the other. To know that even if you don't care about sports, your partner's enthusiasm for them can add to the marriage, even if it only serves to make that one person happier. Good marriages know that both lives are enhanced by the joy that is added to the home, even if it is only one person's joy. It is a matter of attitude. With the right approach it is possible to be enriched by the people your partner likes and you do not, by religious differences, diverse spending habits, political perspectives, sexual pleasures, time priorities, expressions of affection, or personal interests. All that is required is the willingness to say what is important to you and understand what is important to the other and then use those differences as an arena for sensitivity and generosity. When people become evangelists or, what is worse, imperialists who try to convince or force the other into a shared view, the marriage stands in harm's way.

Notice that agreement is not what makes disagreement good. It is fine when people can come to a common view. But it is not always necessary. In an atmosphere of respect and sensitivity agreement is not as important as it is when these qualities are missing or weakened. While there are times when decisions must be made and only one person's view can be honored, contrary views often only need to be respected and taken into account in the future. *Most* reasonable people can meet *most* of their goals in *most* arguments when they are listened to, taken seriously and understood. Unresolved contrary views between people confident of their mutual respect can provide opportunity for generosity and forgiveness which, when given and received in love, are beautiful and solid building blocks for families. The point is that disagreements are not only inevitable in healthy relationships, they can be a vital part of what makes it healthy.

## *Beginning to talk about disagreeing:*

How are we different from one another?

How do those differences show up in our life together?

Where did you learn how to disagree with another person? Home? School? Brothers and sisters? Trial and error while growing up?

How do you like to be treated in a disagreement?

Does the Golden Rule apply in our disagreements? (Reminder: "Do unto others as you would have them do unto you.")

What do we have to learn from each other?

## PRINCIPLE TWELVE

# There is a big difference between a disagreement and a misunderstanding.

### Points of View

**A.** Don't you see what I mean?...What does my weight have to do with it?...Why does every conversation have to end up as a shouting match?...Don't speak to me in that tone of voice...If you would just listen...If I understand you, I agree with part of what you are saying but not all...Why do you keep trying to change the subject?...It really upsets me when you talk about my family that way...

**B.** I am not sure that I understand what you are trying to say...I never said anything about your weight...Slow down and tell me again what you are trying to tell me...That is not the point...I liked it better when you were mumbling. At least then there was a chance you were making sense...I wish we had handled last night's talk a little better. I lost the point and I felt that you did, too...Tell me what you think I am trying to say...

# *Principle*

In a disagreement each knows what the other is trying to say and does not agree with it. In a misunderstanding people do not understand one another and are reacting to messages that are not being sent. Disagreements have the potential to make the relationship stronger by clarifying, enriching, and providing opportunity for affirmation and the positive reinforcement that comes from being listened to and understood. Misunderstandings are heat without light, talk without communication, and emotion without foundation. They have little or no possibility of making things better. Much of the damage done to marriages is done by misunderstandings masquerading as disagreements.

Misunderstandings are insulting because the responses to what one says are rarely appropriate. People tend to feel ignored or attacked. Conversations lose their focus as seemingly extraneous points are made. Arguments slide from subject to subject as both try desperately to say something that will convey their thoughts or feelings. Statements intended to illustrate a point become inflammatory and obscure the original intent with anger. Reason beats a retreat because it has failed to make itself obvious and emotion takes over. Voices get louder as frustration at not being "heard" in the sense of understanding gets treated as the failure to be "heard" in the sense of volume. Attempts to explain what one was trying to say in the first place often trigger the memory of the hurt and anger so that making up becomes more difficult. Agreeing to "forget about it" can be honored by the mind but seldom the heart. The residue of each "forget it" is left in the soul and builds into a nameless hostility. It stays in the background of the marriage until some event brings it out as an anger out of all proportion to the issue at hand. The destructive effect of misunderstandings can linger for years and pollute the environment in which the relationship lives.

The way to turn a misunderstanding into a disagreement is relatively simple. If A can state B's position to B's satisfaction, and vice versa, they can have a disagreement. If either one cannot do it, they are having a misunderstanding. By pausing when they feel the temperature rising in a conversation and seeking such clarity a couple can move from the quicksand of misunderstanding toward the solid ground of disagreement. It is obviously important to do this before people's temperatures get higher than their IQs. It is also a good thing to call a little "time out" in an argument to be sure that each still knows what the other is talking about. Being able to say, "I don't feel understood about this. What do you think I am trying to say?" can do wonders in keeping a discussion on track.

Experience will no doubt tell you that this is not always easy. We are emotional animals. Reason, clear insight into our own motives, and impartial assessment of others are not constant with us. Some would say they are not even possible for us. We get angry. We have buttons that can be pushed on purpose or by accident. There are some topics that are difficult for us. Some of us were taught to rely on volume, sweet talk, or violence more than logic, conversation, and compromise. We have subconscious agendas that show up in our conversations as barbs, threats, and put-downs no matter how pure our conscious intentions may be. We are all capable of "agreement clashes" where we say the same thing in different ways and find ourselves dueling over semantics rather than substance. Alcohol and drugs can produce what some refer to as "stinkin' thinkin'" that distorts any discussion. And we do have bad days, awkward moments and chaotic chemistry. These all help to make destructive misunderstandings out of disagreements or even casual conversation. And they keep us from doing simple, reasonable things like making sure we know what the other person is trying to say before responding.

In spite of these realities there are ways for emotional people like us to keep our eyes on the high ground of reason where our differences are less destructive and more likely to be helpful. The first point is to know that all of us need help in remaining reasonable. Our strongest feelings, our deepest convictions all need to be looked at in the cool light of reason from time to time. The best way to do this is to reflect on arguments after they are over. Not just in one's own mind, but together. Couples who want to make their marriage better can make a point of saying, "How could we have done better in our discussion about $X$ last night?" This gives people a chance to say important things like, "I did not understand what you meant...I was too tired to follow your point...I wish I had not mentioned $Y$ when we were talking about $X$...I was hurt when you said $Z$..."

In such a discussion it is important to speak only of your own reactions, experiences, and feelings. Statements like, "You were being pigheaded," are unfair, to say nothing of unhelpful. Saying, "I did not feel listened to or understood," conveys the same point in language less likely to start the whole thing over again. The point is to reflect on the conversation, not recreate it. This kind of speaking and reflecting on a difficult time in the marriage requires both discipline and practice. The discipline is to use a peaceful moment to revisit a painful one. Few people are eager to do that, but the tranquil moment is the only one in which helpful reflection can take place. Practice is what it takes before people know the right words for their own thoughts and feelings. We are all too quick to judge others and love to assign base motives to those on the other side in an argument. The effect is always to widen rather than bridge the gap between disputants. Speaking of one's own thoughts, feelings, and experiences is worth learning because it is safe and positive. Safe, since you are the only expert in the world on how you think, feel, and experience life. Positive, because a reaction can be described without any element of judgment. Feelings are amoral and come unbidden to a situation. Feeling excluded at a certain point in the conversation is no more a judgment than not liking the color red or being fond of mashed potatoes. A feeling is always innocent. What we do with a feeling is another matter. Feeling excluded is simply a fact of my life. What I might do to get your attention is subject to judgment. In the reflection on an argument it is possible to help one another learn how to speak about one's own experiences and feelings in a manner that will lead to good disagreements and avoid bad misunderstandings.

There is a second point that is important to have in mind when struggling to keep disagreeing without misunderstanding. There can be a difference between what one is trying to say and what one is actually communicating. It is possible, even easy, to communicate something quite different from what one is trying to say. Something playful is heard as threatening, something you thought was funny is found offensive, an attempt to be clear is received as nagging, the desire to resolve is experienced as controlling. Words can touch subjects in the hearer that are unknown to the speaker, a certain tone of voice or inflection can communicate far beyond the scope of the language used. Neither the speaker nor the hearer is likely to be objective about what is being said. The more important or emotional the conversation, the greater the possibility of a gap between what is said and what is heard. Many fine disagreements have fallen into that gap and emerged as furious misunderstandings. There is no known cure. But people who reflect on their arguments can know that such gaps almost always exist, which means that they will not know what happened until they understand what was heard as well as what was said. Knowing what you were trying to say and what you understood the other to be saying is not enough to know about a conversation. We have to know what the other person was trying to say and what he or she understood us to be saying before the picture is complete. Reflective marriages can learn to use or avoid certain words, tones, and inflections in order to communicate effectively during a disagreement. Almost everyone tries to learn that language for making love. It is also handy when making war.

### *Beginning to talk about disagreements and misunderstandings:*

Have you ever been in a conversation where you thought people did not understand what you were trying to say?

What did you do or what would you have liked to do in such a situation?

How do people get better at disagreeing?

What do you expect from people who disagree with you?

It has been said that "a gentlemen is never unintentionally rude." Have you ever been unintentionally rude in a conversation? What happened?

What happens when people "just forget about" an argument?

# Arguments
# are cone-shaped.

## *Points of View*

A. You never listen to me...Can't you see that I am upset?...Don't make jokes. This is no laughing matter...You were ready to hit me!...Just forget it. I will not bring that subject up again...If we are going to talk about church again we had better sit down and deal with it once and for all...Why won't you answer me?...I can't talk about this anymore.

B. Why can't we carry on a civilized conversation about money?...Just tell me how you really feel... We have been putting this off for weeks and now time has run out. We have to do something now!...We are stuck. Let's call that counselor the Browns liked so much...I saw this interview on Oprah where this doctor said that men who behave the way you do are in need of serious help... Can we turn off the TV for a few minutes? I need your full attention...Mary, we need to talk about something.

## Principle

Sometimes a visual image can help us understand the unseen realities of life. Poets and painters, dancers, and sculptors as well as those who choose team mascots have been doing it for years. In the same vein it is possible to represent the dynamic of a disagreement by considering the shape of a cone, which is wide on one end and continually narrows to a closed point.

Disagreements usually begin at the open end where there is the most maneuvering room. The early stage of an argument has options which latter stages lack. People can speak freely without the defensiveness that conflict introduces. Subjects can be dealt with abstractly or even humorously ("How about ear plugs during my mother's visit?"). Delicate topics can be touched upon and revisited at a better time ("We need to finish that conversation about when we make love"). As the discussion continues it moves further into the cone. Ill, or even well-chosen, words serve to limit ones choices for future words. People do not forget words like foolish, typical, immature, or crazy when they are applied to an individual's behavior. The use of absolutes like "always" and "never" tend to dig a hole that makes constructive response difficult, if not impossible. Few people are consistent enough to be *always* or *never* anything. A position taken is not easily abandoned as the conversation moves from the intellectual toward the personal. Time is often a factor and its passage serves to limit options ("The closer the time comes the fewer options we have about what to do when your family comes to visit"). Hurt feelings, frustration, embarrassment, competition, feeling misunderstood, reluctance to admit wrong, exhaustion, and anger all conspire to pull a couple further into the cone where the limited space intensifies emotions while limiting choices. The end of this progression is the closed tip of the cone where progress is not possible. All that can be done then is turn and walk away or break the cone.

Walking away can take a variety of forms. It can be done literally by leaving the room, walking around the block, or some other exercise that allows cooling off so that the conversation can be restarted at a wider point in the cone. People can stop the conversation and get help from a friend or counselor. This is essentially extending the cone by asking a third party to help find options not apparent to the couple. Another, and dangerous, option is to declare a mini-divorce. This is a decision not to talk about this subject again. It establishes an exception to their total commitment by affirming that they are together in all things except this thing. Mini-divorces are an acknowledgment that civil conversation is not possible in a certain area, so the topic will be avoided. When people discover that conversations about money, family, discipline for the children, work, religion, alcohol, or flirtatious relationships always turn into destructive fights, they often choose not to start those conversations in the first place. Why travel a road that experience tells you does not go anyplace you want to be? The danger, of course, is that each mini-divorce is like cutting a strand of a rope. It might be possible to cut one or two but soon the rope is undone. Too many mini-divorces reduce the marriage to pointless chatting about safe subjects, long periods of silence, adulterous relationships where talking is permitted, or the realization that the marriage has died of too many mini-divorces.

Breaking the cone is resorting to violence, which is what people do when they cannot make progress by talking. It is the last resort when all other forms of communication and persuasion have failed, the rebuttal of the inarticulate. Violence is forcing one's will on another, and is the opposite of two wills seeking resolution. There are many among us whose powers of discussion are so limited that they are quickly reduced to shouts, threats, muscle, or weaponry. We mark them as abusers and are rightly concerned about being in relationship with them. They go too quickly from conversation to confrontation, while the rest of us take many steps where there are many opportunities for resolution and reconciliation. It is possible for abusers to be quite patient and articulate in some relationships—business, or society for example—but dangerously limited in the intense intimacy of marriage. The causes are complex and so are the appropriate responses. One thing is obvious. Abuse is what people do when they run out of options. If abusers could change by themselves, they would have done so already. They need outside help.

It should also be noted that abuse is not limited to the physical. People can be brutalized with words as well as hands. Cutting remarks do damage and can be as abusive as a raised fist. Speaking in terms your partner does not understand as well as you do is another form of abuse. Some people lack the language skills to speak of their own emotions; others are frustrated when management theories or religious concepts are introduced. Quoting authors no one else has read, relying on an unnamed "they" to bear witness to a point, assigning motives to others, referring to painful memories, or turning on tears, chest pains, or the ever-popular "I am too tired to talk about it" are all forms of coercion and, therefore, of violence.

Conversations that get away from people and turn into nasty exchanges are those that have slipped into the cone where walking away and violence are more than possible. Marriages that are good at disagreeing understand the dynamic of the cone, know when they are approaching it, and are aware of alternatives.

One alternative is a DEW Line. You may remember that term from the Cold War. It stands for Distant Early Warning and refers to the line of radar installations that were set across the Arctic and other places to give our nation an early notice of incoming missiles. Thankfully it was never necessary in international relations, but it is often necessary in domestic ones. It is important to be able to recognize an argument as, or even before, it begins. Many people do not even know they are having a disagreement until they are far into the cone. I know individuals who did not realize there was a problem in the marriage until their spouse walked out. If people know they are entering that cone they can behave in ways that take advantage of the maneuvering room at the open end. Arguments can be recognized by their subject matter. If you know that it is hard for you to talk about money, for example, then a conversation about finances is potentially the beginning of a trip into the cone. Approach it with caution and use your wisest words. Tone of voice can indicate that a subject is important to the speaker. People can speak in italics, with exclamation points, and with warning labels. Do not miss those signs and take a serious subject lightly. The time of a conversation may indicate its importance. An early riser who stays up late in order to talk, someone comes home early from work, the kids sent off to a movie to allow time for a conversation, or an unusual call made to the office—are all indicators of serious subjects.

Terminology can signify trouble. When I was growing up and my mother referred to me as "young man" I knew I was in trouble. By the same token being called "John" instead of "Jack" or "Jennifer" instead of "Jen" can tip the alert partner to a potentially charged situation.

The DEW Line is not for avoiding conversation but to help people deal constructively with difficult subjects. Once warned, partners can make communication a higher priority than just speaking one's mind. Such situations call for sensitivity to how the other feels about this subject and how the other responds to certain words. The point is not to be false or manipulative but to be effective in communicating. This is not a time for jokes or for sarcasm. In such situations it helps to have a clear goal for the discussion. If you have trouble talking about a family relationship then an unfocused rambling chat about it will probably disappear inside of the cone. Know what needs to be dealt with and keep that in the forefront. Do not go down side roads or succumb to temptations to revisit old battlefields. If you need to discuss a holiday visit, be sure that everything you say has to do with that issue. If possible, know what the end of the conversation will look like. "We are trying to decide how best to spend Thanksgiving with your parents. When we get that figured out, this conversation will be over." That may seem too formal but something like it will keep difficult conversations from becoming impossible ones.

Sometimes a hard subject does not need both statement and rebuttal. It may be enough for one person to state her mind and the other to indicate that he understands what has been said. "I really disagree with your decision to call Junior's teacher about his report card. I wish that we had talked it over beforehand. I would have wanted to talk to

Junior first." In such an instance, the deed is done and cannot be changed. Presumably the reasons for the call have already been expressed. The only response necessary is one of understanding the validity of that point of view and an awareness of it for the future. Rehashing the reasons is not going to do anything but move the marriage down into the cone. If two people have made their point and still do not agree, the focus of the conversation needs to switch from the past to the future. The only question with any hope of making things better is: How will we deal with this situation or these different views in the future? (see Principle Fourteen).

Marriages often find themselves inside the cone because the individuals have different rhythms for dealing with issues. Some people need to talk about their feelings as they are experiencing them. Others like to privately sort through an experience and talk about it later. When two such people marry, they often feel pressured on the one hand or ignored on the other. One seems to go on and on in never-ending circles and the other appears cruelly unresponsive and disinterested. Both perceptions could be true. There are people who love the sound of their own voices and there are others with a dysfunctionally narrow band of interest. They need help beyond the scope of this book. But there are also caring individuals who have different time frames for their minds and hearts. The "what comes up comes out" sort of personality can know that a prolonged monologue is not in the best interests of the marriage and that response to what is said will not be effusive. The person who likes to turn feelings into thoughts before dealing with them can know that his or her partner needs some immediate acknowledgment even if it is only eye contact and occasional indications of understanding. Both need to know that in their marriage such conversations are not over in one sitting. The talker needs to talk and then the thinker needs to come back with a response. Too often the conversation ends when the talker is through or so frustrated by the lack of response that it is called off. In such circumstances the thinker rarely is heard from because there is no easy way to restart the conversation. A healthy couple can know that, as in *Robert's Rules of Order,* a subject can be "postponed to a time certain." This means that everyone agrees that discussion will end but will be continued at a specific later date. A couple can have the talker's part of a conversation and then agree to finish the discussion on Saturday morning or Wednesday at dinner or whenever. It is a little cumbersome, but it is much better than plunging down the inside of a cone simply because two people who love one another have different ways of carrying on a conversation.

Cones can also be avoided by those willing to remember that if something is important to one person, it is important to the marriage. Enormous amounts of negative energy are allowed to build up in a household around different ideas of what is important. Being trivialized by another's lack of interest is deadly poison to a relationship. Efforts to require others to feel as you do about a subject are seldom helpful. What is required is some gift-giving. The gifts are understanding and sensitivity. When one person wants to talk about football or fashion, the neighbors or the Internet, the Gospel or gossip, and the other is not especially interested, a gift can be given. The form of the gift is listening. A wise man named William Stringfellow had this to say about it:

Listening is a rare happening among human beings. You cannot listen to the word another is speaking if you are preoccupied with your appearance or with impressing the other or are trying to decide what you are going to say when the other stops talking or are debating about whether what is being said is true or relevant or agreeable. Such matters have their place, but only after listening to the word as the word is being uttered. Listening is a primitive act of love in which a person gives himself to another's word, making himself accessible and vulnerable to that word.[12]

Another good gift is brevity on the part of the speaker. Because these are gifts, they should be acknowledged. The speaker will probably know that the couple's enthusiasms do not match. The patient listener should be thanked for such generous caring. The good listener can admire the joy or concern that the speaker has. The situation becomes one full of opportunities for affirming their love for each other rather than a slippery walk on the edge of the cone.

[12]William Stringfellow, quoted in *Friends Journal—Quaker Thought and Life Today,* circa 1978-79.

## *Beginning to talk about cones:*

What topics seem difficult for the two of you to talk about?

What are some of the things that make those conversations hard for you?

Do the two of you handle difficult subjects differently?

How would you characterize your way of dealing with those subjects?

If listening is "a primitive act of love," how do you like to be listened to?

What do you want from a loving listener?

Is that what your partner expects from you as a listener or does your partner seem to want something different?

# Pronouns and verbs
# are the longitude and latitude
# of a disagreement.

## *Points of View*

A. We never seem to resolve anything…We have been having the same argument over and over again for years…How we feel at any given moment is not the most important thing about us…Let's talk about how we handled that disagreement about the kids last night… How we decide things is probably more important than what we decide…I do not want to hurt your feelings… Sometimes when we argue I want to laugh at how silly we are being but I think it would just make you angry.

B. We fight like cats and dogs but we always make up so it is OK…I like to get things off my chest…I am not going to let you get away with anything…You say what you want but then do not listen to what I think… Some of the best sex we have is after an argument…Sometimes our arguments are so pointless we cannot remember what they were about.

## *Principle*

Although it is difficult in the heat of an argument to notice things like pronouns and verb tenses, like longitude and latitude they give an accurate indication of where the discussion is at the moment. Couples may only be able to use these indicators while reflecting on a disagreement later, but they are valuable even then.

Singular pronouns and past tense verbs are the language of conflict. When the conversation is sprinkled with "He said...she said...I did *X*...you did *Y*" the couple are in a valuable and necessary stage of disagreeing but little progress is being made. It is an improvement on seething silence, but it is not close to a conclusion much less reconciliation. The best that can be happening is clarification, as each describes the situation from his or her point of view. The other less positive possibility is that accusations are being made. Accusations are seldom if ever helpful because the logical response to attack is defense. The one who feels accused tends to pull away, close whatever openness there might have been, and erect barricades of noise, motion, or silence behind which counterattacks are plotted. The truth has a hard time making it across the no man's land between an accusatory statement and a defensive mind.

Singular pronouns and present tense verbs are an improvement over singular pronouns and past tense verbs. When people begin to speak of how they think or feel in the present, the focus shifts from an unreachable and uncorrectable past to the here and now where love, understanding, and generosity can do their work. "I feel betrayed" (present tense) is far more open and welcoming than "You betrayed me" (past tense). "I am hurt" (or angry, or frustrated, or disappointed) invites many more positive responses than the past tense accusatory "You hurt my feelings." "I do not want to hurt you" or "I am trying to do what I think is best" or "I am confused by my own actions" are all present tense statements with potential for healing. Sharing one's current thoughts and feelings is an act of vulnerability that invites the better instincts of both partners to be expressed. Such personal openness requires both tact and courage. The right words that reveal without accusing must be used. And the possibility that the other person will misuse the moment by ignoring or abusing the revelation must be faced.

Singular pronouns and present tense verbs are signs of the beginning of healing. Important as they are, they do not complete the process. Couples who clear the air by getting things off their chest, saying what is on their mind, and letting their feelings out have laid a foundation. They have not built a bridge. The language that makes a bridge between people is plural pronouns and future tense verbs.

When the accusatory "You" + past tense verb (You said...You did...You put...You took...) turns into the vulnerable "I" + present tense verb (I think...I feel...I wonder...) there is progress. The healing is not completed, however, until there are "We" + future tense verb statements (We will...We hope that...We want to...We shall...). Agreeing on how a couple will respond to similar circumstances in the future turns a dispute into a healthy investment. Establishing the appropriate response to anticipated words or actions makes a relationship more solid and secure. Mature, educated marriages are able to say, "The next time this comes up, we will handle it this way." Disagreements are good when they provide lessons that make the relationship stronger. Agreeing on how the marriage will be better because of what was learned from the dispute is what reconciliation is all about.

It is good to confront and healthy to disagree. It is positive to be open about one's thoughts and feelings. But life only goes in one direction, and that is into the future. Reconciliation always faces the future. Many otherwise healthy marriages get into trouble because they do not manage to get their disagreements all the way home to reconciliation. Making up is a form of truce, a decision that other things are more important or interesting or fun than fighting. Reconciliation is coming to agreement about the future. When people fail to reach reconciliation two symptoms are often present. Arguments get repeated over and over. Or arguments slide from one topic to another. For example, a couple will disagree about going out with friends. When this heats up a little, someone reminds the other that they behaved badly at the family Thanksgiving Dinner last year, whereupon the accused notes that the accuser has never mastered the checkbook, and so on. These extraneous topics are available to be used as weapons in the current conflict because they were not resolved. The way to be sure that conflicts are resolved and not just set aside is to reflect on the conversation after it is over and passions have cooled. It is a difficult but important thing to do because, in spite of our devotion to the idea that experience is a great teacher, no one ever learns by experience alone. One learns by reflecting on experience. (See Principle Twelve for the importance of reflection on arguments and disagreements.)

## *Beginning to talk about resolving disagreements:*

Do you feel that your disputes get resolved?

Recall a recent disagreement. How could you have handled it differently?

Do disagreements ever repeat themselves in your relationships?

Do arguments ever "slide"?

Do your disagreements ever get stuck in past tense or present tense verbs?

Is there a difference in your mind between making up and reconciliation?

## PRINCIPLE FIFTEEN

# Forgiveness takes effort.

### *Points of View*

**A.** I'm sorry...I did not mean it...I know, I know. I should have known better...It was not my fault...Lots of people do that and worse...It won't happen again...I said I am sorry. What more do you want from me?...I can't take your holier-than-thou attitude...What about the time when you...Everybody makes mistakes... Let's just forget about it and go on.

**B.** Haven't we had this conversation before?...I know I should forgive and forget...This is becoming a pattern...I cannot trust you until you prove yourself trust-worthy...You have gone too far this time...You are just taking me for granted...It does not just go away because you say that you are sorry...How can I forgive you over and over?...This is not working...You need to get some help.

### *Principle*

While specifics vary among individuals, it is safe to say that the people we love include the following in their makeup: dishonesty, unfairness, errors, self-absorption, defensiveness, distraction, insensitivity, a tendency toward destruction, impurity, limitations, prejudices, inconsistencies, rudeness, vanity, corruption, impulsiveness, stubbornness, and occasional thoughts that would embarrass the Marquis de Sade. To make matters worse it is also safe to say that we, too, share those traits. While these characteristics may not define us, they are present in us all. The religious word for this reality is "sinfulness." The secular word is "human nature." No matter what it is called, it makes forgiveness an essential part of any lifelong relationship.

Forgiveness is also important because, as was noted earlier, we are not made for each other. We do not fit exactly together. There are gaps of viewpoint, under-standing, priority, and principle. The "angels of our better nature" that Lincoln urged people to rely on do not always hold sway. And there are forces in this world that seem to complicate the simple, magnify the wrong, obscure the obvious, and convert our good intentions into paving stones on the road to hell. These things require forgiveness to be near the center of all our relationships and at the center of our households.

Forgiveness joins what is separated by life. It makes possible what our sinful human nature conspires to make impossible. It removes barriers so that life can go on. It is the mortar for our brick, the stitch for our hem, the margin for our error. It is the duct tape of life. No marriage can survive without it. Because of all of this, it is important to know what forgiveness is and is not, to know how it works and how it is done.

Forgiveness is not justification nor is it acceptance. Both of these ways of responding to issues have a key role to play in relationships and are often thought to be forgiveness, but they are not. Justification takes something that was understood to be wrong and reverses that judgment. The usual method is by way of explanation. You thought we were to meet at the corner of Third and Main at 4 p.m. and when I did not show up, you were angry with me. I am able to explain that I was waiting for you at the corner of Fourth and Main at 3 p.m. Clearly there was a misunderstanding so my absence can be justified. I did not just fail to do what I promised, I did what I thought I had agreed to do. We may have to work on communication or I may owe you an apology for not paying attention to the details, but the offense of standing you up is removed by being justified, explained away. Forgiveness is not needed.

Acceptance is another common response that can easily be mistaken for forgiveness. It is the willingness of the offended party to live with (accept) the reality of the offensive behavior. You came to the corner of Third and Main at 4 p.m., and I was thirty minutes late. I explain that I tried to get there on time but just could not make it. It would be far better if I were able to change my ways and keep my appointments, but for the sake of this illustration we will assume that I cannot. The issue will either be a bone of continuing contention between us or you will accept my shortcoming and we will move on to other things. You agree to accept the fact that I am probably going to be late for any appointment we have and adjust your expectations accordingly. Such acceptance affirms that our relationship is more important than this failure of mine, and the offended party makes the required adjustment to keep it from being an ongoing fight that spoils our time together. Acceptance is a valuable gift to give in a relationship and it should be appreciated by the one who receives it even as the one who gives it needs to be sure he or she can afford it. If it is not appreciated, the giver feels used. If it is more of a gift than the emotions of the giver can afford, that is, if you are going to be seething with anger every time I am late but covering it up with a smile, it lays groundwork for continuing resentment which undermines the relationship. Acceptance does not necessarily mean that you are happy about my shortcomings but it does mean that you will be able to keep your feelings about them from polluting our relationship. Important as this is, it is still not forgiveness.

Forgiveness is unique. It is a gift that can be given when justification or acceptance are not possible. The gift is given by the offended and must be accepted gratefully by the offender. It involves both the offender and the offended acting as if something did not happen even though they both know it did. It is not being dishonest but is choosing to move from an unhealthy place in the relationship to a healthy one. It takes effort on the part of both partners. The classic formula involves three parts: an event and repentance and forgiveness. The *event* is the missed appointment at Third and Main. The fact is that I was playing solitaire and did not leave on time because I was winning. I cannot justify my actions because there is no reasonable explanation. You are, understandably, unwilling to accept such behavior as a continuing fact of our relationship. I *repent* (the word literally means "to go in a new direction" and in this sense it refers to changed behavior) by saying that I am sorry and will not do it again. Your *forgiveness* means that you will treat me as if this never happened, even though we both know that it did. The next time we have an appointment you will show up on time with every expectation that I will do the same. I will make my repentance real by tearing myself away from the lures of solitaire and keeping the appointment.

Forgiveness is about the way we will live together in the future in spite of the way we have lived together in the past. It discounts the past in order to free the future. The process may be simple but what it requires is profound. Repentance is more than feeling sorry about something, and forgiveness is more than withholding punishment. The offender must make a commitment to changed behavior in the future. The offended must go against the instinct to avoid being hurt again and remain open, trusting, and vulnerable. Forgiveness is risky business. Failure brings renewed and multiplied pain. The little example of the missed meeting at Third and Main, unless it is part of a pattern of neglect, is probably not the kind of situation that demands the difficult choices and chances of serious forgiveness. It is important, however, that couples practice on little events so that they will have skills in place for the challenge of dealing with the emotionally charged core issues of a shared life. If forgiveness is not worked out in little things like missed appointments, there is scant hope that it will be possible in big things like adultery or dishonesty. Successful forgiveness brings a renewed and multiplied joy. It is worth practicing.

While the work of forgiveness must be undertaken by both, there are special responsibilities laid on the offended one. The first has to do with rebuilding trust. The offender cannot prove trustworthy until given something to be trustworthy about. Trust cannot be established in theory or exercised in a vacuum. The offended one has to become vulnerable to the offender before he or she can demonstrate that the previous behavior has changed. The thief must be trusted with money, the adulterer with relationships, and the liar with information. No healing, no new way of perceiving one another can happen until this takes place. In many circumstances it can be very difficult and not everyone gets it right the first time. The offender needs to be patient as the offended struggles to be open once again. The second burden on the forgiver is the moral sense that one "ought" to forgive because it is the decent thing to do. Christians have the specific teaching of Jesus who, when asked whether one should forgive another as often as seven times, said that we should forgive seventy times seven. This is not meant to set the magic number at 490, but to indicate that forgiveness is a continuing process in human relationships. Other traditions have similar concepts.

Experience as well as faith would tell us that forgiveness is a constant in healthy relationships since we all need some degree of it all of the time. But offended persons often feel the full weight of the call to be forgiving while struggling with pain and disappointment, and can be pressured into accepting repentance that is not real or extending a promise of continuing trust that they cannot maintain. Forgiveness that heals does not come about under such duress. While forgiveness should be continuous it need not be mindless. Healthy people do not accept promises they do not believe nor do they make promises they cannot keep. For repentance to be real, the behavior must be controllable. If the offenses grow out of illness or dysfunction, it is foolish to think that remorse and a promise to do better will make any difference. Addictions to alcohol, or drugs, or uncontrollable violence are sadly common examples of this situation. Repentance also requires will power. If the will to change is lacking, no promise will be kept for long. Some people are just not ready to grow up and leave adolescent antics or the comfort of parental intervention. In such cases there are two options: accept the behavior or get help on how to deal with it. It is also foolish to promise forgiveness if there is no commitment to trust and vulnerability. Why say, "I forgive you" when the real message is "I cannot trust you"? Perhaps the honest and most helpful response would be, "I want to forgive you and trust you again, but right now I cannot. Please be patient with me while I work on it." In such circumstances working on it means cooling off, thinking things over, talking with some trusted people, and trying to come to the view that the future of the relationship is more important than its past.

We love to repeat the old saying, "Forgive and forget." As with most such bumper sticker statements it is true as far as it goes, but it does not go very far. There are many bumps and bruises in life that are forgettable and should be. But there are also injuries that cannot be easily set aside. Those who try to forgive too quickly or without sufficient thought are enabling and supporting behaviors that are not good for the relationship. Such a person may feel kind-hearted, but is joining in the undermining of the marriage. These times call for a deeper understanding of forgiveness and the hard work that it requires. When repentance and forgiveness are needed for the relationship, but the couple is stuck in denial or anger, it is not time to give up. It is time to get help. If you do not know where to go for help, call a church and ask whom they recommend for marriage counselors. If they do not know, call another church until you get an answer.

## A refresher on justification, acceptance, and forgiveness:

**Justification**: John is seen by his wife in a restaurant with an attractive woman. When asked about it John explains that it was his client's wife. The client joined them later for lunch. The situation is justified by the explanation.

**Acceptance**: Sharon leaves clothes all over the bedroom which irritates Paul. After many arguments he determines that she is not likely to change. Paul accepts the role of tidying the bedroom in order to avoid fruitless confrontation.

**Forgiveness**: Mike calls to say he must work late and so must miss their two-year-old's birthday party. Actually he went to the ball game with his friends. Susan finds out about it and is very angry and disappointed. Mike agrees that he behaved badly and promises not to do so again. Susan forgives him. Three months later Mike calls to say that he must work late and miss having dinner with Susan's parents. Old memories and hurts flare up in Susan's mind but in the name of forgiveness she ignores them and accepts Mike's explanation. Mike, aware of his obligations as a forgiven person, leaves work as soon as he can and joins his in-laws for dessert.

## *Beginning to talk about forgiveness:*

How did forgiveness work in the home where you grew up?

What makes forgiveness hard to give?

What makes forgiveness hard to accept?

Can the future of a relationship be more important than its past?

How does trust get built in a relationship? Can it be rebuilt in the same way?

# GOOD GLUE

# Routine maintenance is as important for a marriage as it is for a car.

## *Points of View*

A. I never know what is going on with you…Are you ignoring me?…I know you love me but for the life of me I do not know why you love me or how you are doing it…We have to clear the air…It seems like you just do whatever you want whenever you want to do it…I feel like I am all alone in this marriage…How was I to know that you were upset about the loan?…It seems as if everything we do is routine. What happened to our special times?… The only time you talk is when you want something. I feel manipulated…Do you love me?

B. Actions speak louder than words…It is hard for me to describe how I feel…If you loved me you would know…Quit bugging me all of the time. I need some peace and quiet…Can't you tell?…The only time we are really honest with each other is when we are arguing…Of course I love you. Nothing has changed.

# *Principle*

If you have ever purchased a new car, you know that they always give you a maintenance schedule about changing the oil, rotating the tires, and checking the belts at certain times. The clear implication is that no matter how wonderful the car looks, smells, handles, and runs at the day of purchase, it will be a pile of junk in a few years if the routine maintenance does not take place. If we only change the oil when the dashboard light comes on or if we only rotate the tires when one of them goes flat, we cannot expect the car to last very long. Routine maintenance is an understood part of having a new car. Somehow we have failed to extend this obvious point to include marriage even though the family is intended to last much longer and is known to be more complex than an automobile.

Marriages need maintenance. If the only time people talk about their relationship is when they are arguing or making up, they cannot expect it to last long. If the only words heard about how they are perceived by their partner are in the context of sexual passion, the words will lose their power. If people only think about the health of a relationship when their feelings are hurt, the joy will slip away. If a couple believes that their love for one another is so firm that it does not need discussion, they will find that what goes without saying usually just goes away. That is why marriages need routine maintenance.

Maintenance is a notably unromantic word: It is not about finding time to be alone, or flirting, or enjoying the delights of mutual seduction. Maintenance is about putting feelings into words. It is allowing one person to see what is going on inside of the other. To be specific, it means taking five minutes every week or so to tell your partner what it feels like to be in the relationship. The time should be scheduled so that it is natural and easily remembered. Before dinner on payday, the first of the month, Sunday before church, or Saturday morning are all recognizable and regularly recurring times when these conversations can happen. To keep the ten-minute limit it is wise to have the maintenance session just before something else that will make it easy to stop the discussion. Most of the people I know go to church (not unnatural when you consider my line of work), so a good time for them is on their way to Sunday services. They can have the maintenance but will drop it as they greet others and begin worship. There is also an extra bonus in the quiet time church offers to reflect on what has been heard. If church is not part of your life you might consider starting the maintenance session ten minutes before your favorite TV show or on your way to work if you travel together. Walking or jogging is another possibility. One very successful method suggests writing a note to your spouse each night before going to bed. If all else fails, set a timer. Do not worry that everything does not get said in a maintenance session. Keep it short and easy or our natural human reluctance to deal with difficult topics will invent a thousand reasons not to do it.

It is important that the speaker talk only about his or her feelings because feelings are neutral. People cannot control how they feel about something; we can only control what we do when we have the feeling. This marks an important distinction between thoughts and feelings. Thoughts can be negotiated like labor disputes. They can be discussed and changed by reason, argument, and discovery. Feelings must be navigated like a river. People often say that a person should not feel a certain way. That is an oxymoron. There is no "should" to feelings. They simply exist and cannot be moved by logic or debate. Individuals and couples have to find a way to get where they want to be by dealing with feelings, not by changing them. While talking about feelings we cannot "should" on each other. Another reason for speaking in terms of one's feelings is that the speaker is the only person in the world who knows what his or her feelings are. No one can correct you when you are talking about how you feel because nobody but you knows what those feelings are.

In maintenance sessions it is important to include positive feelings in the comments. If it is all negative, the sessions will become painful and will be avoided. Remember that negatives make more of an impression than positives. If John says to Mary, "You are lovely, gracious, kind, and gentle, but your eyes look a little funny," Mary will be devastated. In a sentence like that the word "but" works like multiplying by zero in math; it wipes out everything that has gone before. It is the negative comment that sticks in the mind of the hearer. For this reason it is good advice to end a statement of feelings with an emphasis on the positive.

The listener's role is simply to listen, saying no more than "I see," or "I understand," or "I did not know that." Be careful about asking for clarification as it can easily lead to an argument. "What do you mean by that?" can be heard as an accusation, especially when the speaker is trying to make a difficult point or address a delicate subject. The point is to try to understand what your partner is experiencing so that you can love your partner more wisely, more deeply, and with greater sensitivity.

It is not a time to blow off steam, get revenge, or make points. Maintenance sessions are not for problem solving. The purpose is to give people who love one another a chance to put feelings into words in a nonthreatening atmosphere and to hear as clearly as possible what is in the heart and mind of the other. If the feelings described point to an issue that needs to be addressed, a separate time should be established for talking about it.

Because the concept of maintenance for a marriage is probably a new one, let me try to illustrate what a maintenance session might be like. It is payday when Fred and Martha have agreed to do the maintenance. They stand in the kitchen for a few minutes after dinner and have their discussion. They have found that their routine is to spend evenings in the TV room, so it is easy to have their "maintenance discussions" while cleaning up the kitchen and marking the conclusion by sitting down and turning on the TV. In this way the maintenance remains short and focused. It is Fred's turn to go first.

*Fred:* I really feel pretty good about how things are going with us. I appreciated the support you have given me while we were having so much tension at the office. I am glad that you did not ask me to describe every detail when I came home. I think you would like to know, but I think you know that I do not like to go over those things. I really felt your support. I feel like I have not been as responsive to you in the past few days. I have needed you and have not had much energy to return. I still need more time to work this out in my own mind and I do need some quiet time here at home. Sometimes I have felt that you were anxious about me when I was quiet and kept asking me if I was OK. I just needed the quiet. I really appreciate the space you are giving me though.

*Martha:* Thanks. I see what you mean about asking how you are doing…I have felt really cut out during this time. I know that it is the way it has to be for now, but I cannot help the feeling. I want to be supportive but I wish there were something that I could do. Maybe there isn't anything, but I do not like just standing by. It makes me feel good to know that you appreciate what I am trying to do. I am also worried about my parents and the kind of crabbing they do about each other when I talk to them on the phone. I feel helpless there, too. It is a frustrating time for me.

*F:* I know what you mean. Thanks for letting me know about it.

In this discussion there are plenty of places where Fred or Martha might have made the mistake of trying to deal with what was being said instead of just listening. Martha could have gotten defensive about his notion that she was interrupting his silence or Fred could have tried to respond to her feeling of being "cut out." By just listening they are each prepared to address those issues where it matters most, in the day-to-day life that they share. Fred might make a point of trying to tell Martha more about what is going on at the office and, if appropriate, ask for her advice. When he does, a wise Martha will tell him that she appreciates the effort. Martha might try to learn the difference between Fred's needed quiet when he is gaining strength and the kind of quiet that is just a hole in the conversation that can be filled with talk. An informed Fred might say something like, "Thanks for letting me brood a little this evening." He might remember to ask about Martha's next conversation with her parents, and Martha can encourage Fred by being especially responsive to the "energy" he does bring to the relationship. A secondary benefit of the maintenance session is that it helps the speaker as well as the listener to know what is going on. Quite often we are not sure of our own feelings until we try to put them into words. Turning vague feelings into specific words like "anger," "fear," "gladness," and "sadness" is an illuminating, though often difficult, exercise. The net result of all of this is helping two people who love one another to do it better.

That is an example of how maintenance works and what it does. It is not dramatic. It might not even be memorable. When there is no presenting issue, such as tension at the office, it can focus on liking the way the chicken was cooked or preferring the previous brand of soap that was in the bathroom. There is also room for large issues like not feeling heard or appreciated, being jealous, or concerned about the role of alcohol in the family. Maintenance does not require great skill in expression or deep insight. The words may be awkward or difficult. Like making love or making pizza, thoughtful people can get better at it and everyone knows that reality and perfection do not often meet. Some things in life are worth doing badly. Talking with someone you love is one of them. When a person tries to speak honestly and another tries to listen generously, good things happen.

When a mechanic looks under the hood of the car or a doctor performs a routine examination, an accountant reviews the books or a teacher administers a test, they are all doing the work of maintenance. They are trying to find out the truth about this car, body, account, or student so that the car, body, account, or student can keep doing what it was made, created, established, or enrolled to do. The maintenance of a marriage has the same purpose. People work to bring their own feelings up from the subconscious to the conscious, and then into words, which enable them to know what is going on inside themselves. The partner listens in order to understand what the other is experiencing, so that each can love the other better. The truth is revealed and the marriage is better able to do what it is supposed to do. In case you have forgotten, the purpose of marriage is to make life better. The purpose of maintenance is to help it do just that.

## *Beginning to talk about maintenance:*

What did you talk about before you were married?

Do you listen to each other as well as you used to?

If you had a maintenance time in your marriage, when might it be?

What day of the week or month?

What time of the day?

If you had a couple of minutes to say how you feel about being in this relationship, what would you say first?

If you spoke freely about how you felt about being in this relationship, could you trust your partner to just listen and learn?

# Religion
# makes a difference.

## Points of View

A. I go to church but it does not seem to make any difference…I am trying to be open to what God is doing in my life…If religion is so important to so many people, shouldn't we try to find out why?…"I believe, Lord. Help my unbelief" (Mark 9:24)…I pray for you all of the time but you still do not change…I have felt something with real power brush against my life…I am finding that I can live into my hopes in a way that really makes a difference in my life…

B. I am just not religious…All those people want is your money…I don't have time for that stuff…Oh, sure. I believe in God…I try to lead a good life…You mean that if I just close my eyes and talk, something good will happen? Sounds like mumbo jumbo to me…Church used to mean a lot to me but I guess I outgrew it or something…Something is missing in my life…

# *Principle*

You must be reminded and warned as you read this section that I am a committed Christian. Religion (a belief system) and faith (acceptance of belief) are very important to me and my understanding of all of life, including marriage. I did, however, promise at the beginning to keep the focus on marriage itself rather than on what might make it Christian. I intend to keep that promise, but one cannot look closely and honestly at marriage without considering its religious dimension. Most marriage ceremonies are religious. The covenant (agreement) between the couple and God is one of the things that distinguish marriage from other forms of love and commitment. It is, unfortunately, very easy to miss what is being said about that relationship with God as many weddings trivialize into well-photographed costume epics and semantic bubble baths full of strange and apparently empty words. But all those words and symbols have something to say about being married. They have been fashioned over four thousand years of human experience, and are probably worth considering. We have already talked about the meaning of the promises (see Principle Four). This piece is about two very basic points—a relationship with God and prayer—and how they can make a difference in a lifelong relationship.

Every religion I know of that considers God to be knowable and interested in people's lives (the theological word for it is "immanent") agrees on a basic point. God calls people beyond themselves. Religious traditions and lore are full of accounts of God moving, pulling, pushing, tricking, scaring, teaching, encouraging, and leading people into extending themselves, into giving of themselves. God's constant work with people is to uncurl us, to move us from ego-centeredness to God-centeredness, to bring us from the narrow little world of self-interest to the wider, healthier world of commitment to others. The gifts and blessings of God, unlike the videos we rent, are not intended for our personal entertainment but are meant to equip us for the journey outward. The details vary across a wide range of human and divine experiences, but the dynamic is always the same. God moves us toward something greater than ourselves.

Since this is God's track record as recorded by a variety of observers, it can reasonably be said that being in a relationship with God is being subject to, or at least vulnerable to, that self-giving impulse. It is on this point that the dynamic of marriage and the dynamic of religion begin to work together. Marriage is a self-giving relationship (see Principle Two). The only time marriage works anywhere near its capacity is when each is trying to serve the other, to seek what is best for the other, to become a gift for the other. It is hard to do and we are easily distracted from it. We curl up into our own interests, fold in on our own comfort, preoccupy ourselves with getting what we want. We get tired or frightened, bored or greedy, lazy or ambitious. For these and a thousand more reasons it is difficult for us to keep the "other-centeredness" that a healthy marriage requires. A great deal, perhaps even all, of marriage trouble and failure stems from some form of self-centeredness.

Therefore, doesn't it make sense to have something at the heart of a couple's life that works to remind them of that important, basic, and so easily forgotten point? Doesn't it work for the benefit of the marriage if there is something moving, pulling, pushing, tricking, scaring, teaching, encouraging, and leading people to do the work of marriage? Doesn't it make sense that a good relationship with God, who calls and equips us to care for others, will make us better marriage partners and, thereby, give us better marriages?

I think it does.

I am not so naive as to believe that religious people have good marriages and non-religious people have bad ones. I am not talking about the "one thing" that makes marriages work. I am saying that a healthy relationship with God can have an enormous and positive impact on a marriage. That simple truth is the reason most of our weddings are religious ceremonies and even civil marriages tend to borrow language from the religious traditions. People have known for four thousand years that a good relationship with God and a good marriage go hand in hand.

The second point is about prayer and how it can provide direct support for a marriage. There is much to know about prayer and there are none of us who could not improve our skills. In this regard it is like singing. All of us can do it, some can do it very well, but any of us could learn to do it better. A treatise on prayer is beyond the scope of this book, but there is a basic reality about it that has a particular implication for marriage. Anyone can take advantage of this benefit, no matter what his experience level as a person of prayer, and all of us can improve to take better advantage of it.

The point is that regularly praying for someone removes the destructive power of any anger we might have toward that person.

In this context praying for someone means seeking

God's help in providing that which is best for them. Praying "for" someone is different from praying "at" them. We pray "at" someone when we lobby God to take up our side of a difference. "O Lord, help John to get his head screwed on straight and see that he is being stubborn" is not praying "for" John as much as it is praying "at" him. A prayer "for" John and the marriage might be: "O Lord, John and I are having trouble dealing with this situation; help me to be part of your response to him. Please help both of us to seek and find your will for us." Such prayers are not about changing someone to better suit your own desires. Prayer opens doors that either the "prayor" or the "prayee" may enter. More often than not it is the one who prays who experiences the most change.

Like conversation, prayer should not be used only in case of emergency. If we pray for someone regularly we will be better able to pray for that person during a hard time. If a couple only talk seriously about their relationship when they are fighting, it is not likely that they will ever do a good job of it. Those who talk about their relationship when they are at their best find that they have some helpful resources to draw upon when they are at their worst. The same is true with prayer. If we only pray when we are frightened or angry (sometimes called "foxhole religion") our prayers are not likely to be very effective. Pray regularly and give yourself a chance to get good at it.

The effect of prayer on anger needs to be understood. It does not mean that we will not have anger. Sometimes we do get angry at John and his behavior. The point is that prayer makes it hard to maintain "destructive anger." Anger is a valuable emotion in that it provides focus, creates energy, keeps us honest, and gives an alarm when something is wrong in a relationship. It is only valuable, however, for short periods of time. Sustained anger turns into a toxic bitterness that pollutes the whole relationship. Over the long haul, it cripples and distorts personalities, blocks the avenues for growth and new experience, and makes those who bear it brittle and fragile. When it is maintained, anger becomes a destructive cancer threatening both individuals and relationships. Praying regularly for one's partner can keep anger from metastasizing, the word used to describe cancer that has begun to spread through the body.

Prayer can keep anger focused on its subject and does not allow it into the broader dimensions of the relationship. The self-righteousness ("what makes him so stupid that he cannot see it my way?") that anger encourages is hard to maintain before God. The simplifying ("she just wants her own way") and diminishing ("he doesn't care about anything") of the other that anger suggests is brought into a different focus in the context of prayer. Like profanity or manipulative plots, words of anger, spoken to God in prayer, are quickly recognized as inappropriate. When prayer reveals that anger has finished its usefulness, the bearer has to move on to the healthier and more important question of figuring out what to do about the cause of the anger. Prayer can help there too, but that takes us beyond the focus of this section. The point here is that regularly praying for someone can keep anger from being destructive by moving us on to more constructive thoughts and emotions.

I am a religious man, but this is not intended to be a book about religion. It is about marriages and some principles that can help them to last for a lifetime.

None of the principles is incompatible with religion and could easily have been written with reliance on theological terms. However, the idea has been to write them so that everyone could use them. In that spirit, it has to be noted that the concepts and language of faith are so much a part of our understanding of marriage that it would be foolish to avoid them altogether. The principles of marriage are also based on experience. And human experience includes what has commonly been interpreted as religious experience. At the center of that language and those interpretations are two distinct points: a healthy relationship with God moves people to the kind of self-giving behavior that makes relationships better; and praying for people makes destructive anger difficult, if not impossible, to maintain.

## *Beginning to talk about religion and prayer:*

What has been your experience with religion?

Do you believe in God? If so, what do you believe?

What do you suppose God believes about you?

Have you ever felt that God had any real interest in your life?

Have you ever wanted God to offer something that would make your life better?

What do you expect of your faith?

# WHY BOTHER?

If you have read this far, you may begin to feel like the seven-year-old who was asked whether it was better to be married or single. He said, "It gives me a headache to think about that stuff. I'm just a kid. I don't need that kind of trouble." Marriage can certainly look like nothing but trouble if all one sees is the effort it takes. Commitments and promises, sex and money, children and family, disagreements and maintenance can combine to make a daunting picture. I doubt that anyone ever approached or spent much time in marriage without wondering whether it was worth the trouble. It is! The overwhelming response to the question, "Is it better to be married?" that echoes down through the ages and in hearts and homes everywhere is, "Yes. A good marriage takes effort but it is worth it." Your experience will undoubtedly add significantly to what follows, but here are a few of the reasons lifelong commitments are worth the trouble it takes to establish and maintain them.

The first obvious point is that we need one another. It is not just that we need someone to button the back of a blouse or tell us if our tie looks right. The intimate part of our lives needs an intimate partner just as our business life needs business partners. That need is built into us and our experience as humans. Indeed, the first message of life is one of needing other people. Before birth we live in what is experienced as an autonomous life. The unborn child in a quiet and darkened womb has no awareness of its dependency on the mother. Its needs are met without effort except for the occasional kick to prod its host into a different position. All of that changes in a traumatic and unexplained moment. At birth each of us is assaulted by light, sound, and intervening hands. Food that used to arrive by an uncomplaining umbilical cord now must be coaxed from other people. Warmth that previously maintained itself somewhere near an ideal 98.6° becomes a bewildering function of blankets, arms, and silly clothing all controlled by other people. Bodily functions introduce the heretofore unknown reality of discomfort and further underline the need for other people. Toys and touches, soothing sounds and places to sleep, fresh air and life itself are all in the hands of other people. The overwhelming message of birth is that we cannot do it alone. We need others.

We spend the rest of our lives dealing with variations on that initial discovery. At every age, including the one you are in now, people must ponder and experiment with the question of how to get what we need from the world around us. Infancy focuses on food and sleep; childhood adds an emphasis on discovery; puberty introduces a whole new dimension. Teenagers learn about peers; young adults wrestle with responsibility; middle-aged people grapple with meaning; and the elderly slowly bring the issue full circle with final concerns for food and sleep. Nobody ever gets it all settled. We continue dealing with the issues of childhood when we enter puberty. Grown-ups struggle with the same relationship issues as adolescents. We are just (hopefully) more sophisticated and successful in the ways we work them out. The basic question of how we get what we need from others remains with us from the moment of birth to the moment of death.

Unfortunately, some people only learn to manipulate others. The technique may vary from crying to bullying, threatening to seducing, buying to pleading, but the primitive approach of infancy remains. Others discover the wonderful secret that giving is the key to getting. The greatest lovers, physically, emotionally, intellectually, and socially, are the ones who have learned to get pleasure by giving it. The happiest marriages involve people who know that self-giving is what makes it work. The point is nowhere more eloquently expressed than in the prayer normally attributed to St. Francis, which asks that "we may not so much seek to be consoled as to console; to be understood as to understand; to be loved as to love. For it is in giving that we receive; it is in pardoning that we are pardoned..." Most of us wander around somewhere between poles of total manipulation and self-giving love. But our best moments come when we are loving in the way that St. Paul described for the Christians in Corinth: with a love that is "patient...kind...not envious or boastful or arrogant. It does not insist on its own way; it is not irritable or resentful...It bears all things, believes all things, hopes all things, endures all things" (1 Corinthians 13:4-7).

What we are dealing with at every age as we struggle to get what we need and wander back and forth between primitive manipulation and self-giving love is our need for one another. In many ways satisfying our need for satisfying relationships is the business of life. It is the work of a lifetime in that it takes all of our lives to do it, and in that no life can be considered successful when it is not done well.

The lifelong commitment of marriage is the deepest possible response to that basic human need. It scratches an itch that is deep within us, very close to the heart of life. Being loved is a vital human experience. But being loved by someone who knows us completely adds a dimension that can only be imagined by those innocent of the experience. The traumatic messages of birth that are imbedded so deeply in our minds are soothed by the commitment of a spouse. The primal need for support, touch, and care are eased in a loving household. A lifelong relationship of growing maturity and deepening intimacy provides a satisfying center that enhances every aspect of life and is threatened by nothing in life and keeps all that is not at the center in healthy perspective. Lovers who venture into the world from the base of a good marriage have a confidence, a resource, and a reason that loners must lack.

A second reason for marriage is its beauty. Just as architects have a way of making heating ducts look like works of art and directors can make scenery shifts part of a dance routine, God has a way of covering the necessities of life in beauty. Birds go about the serious business of establishing their territory by chirping the songs we love to hear. Flowers attract life-giving pollen carriers with the smells and colors we enjoy so much. In the same way, our need for one another finds expression in wondrous beauty. The psalmist celebrates, "O how good and pleasant it is when people live together in unity. It is like fine oil upon the head that runs down upon the beard…" (Psalm 133). The ballad wonders, "Do I love you because you're beautiful/ Or are you beautiful because I love you?"[13] To love and to be loved is the most beautiful experience in life.

The Greeks were very wise about the word "love." Where we have only the one word to describe our fondness for everything from God to french fries, they had four different words to cover the richness of love. *Eros*

---

[13]Oscar Hammerstein II, "Do I Love You Because You're Beautiful?" (1957).

referred to romantic love and is the basis for our word "erotic." *Philios*, to which Philadelphia is indebted, represented friendship. *Storge* is a less familiar word that reminds us of the deeply satisfying love of the familiar, a favorite chair, a routine or tradition, a place we return to over and over, an old friendship. *Agape* was the word for the self-giving love that is characteristic of God and the highest achievement of humans. A good marriage is a rich combination of all four in one relationship. Marriage is romantic and sexual, it is friendly and playful, generous and divine. Even that which becomes predictable can be loved with its own satisfactions that function like the bass notes that hold music together or the sound of surf that eases a tired mind. Marriage is friendship undergirded by commitment, painted by experience, and lit by the future. Marriage is where we have opportunity to love and be loved freely in something like the way that God and the best of us do it. The beauty of those four kinds of love all perking at once in the small world of two people makes marriage as different from every other relationship as a feast is from a snack, a stream from a glass of water. In a word (or five), there is nothing like it.

It has been said that a bachelor knows as much about life as a goldfish does about oceanography. While that may be a little overstated, it does make a point. Marriage is a unique experience of life. It involves a depth of knowing that is impossible in any other context. Facades cannot be maintained in a lifetime of day-to-day living. Dishonesty will have the light of truth on it sooner or later. Strengths and weaknesses, courage and cowardice, assets and liabilities, brilliance and foolishness, kindness and cruelty will all have their day because they are all in every one of us. There are no places outside of marriage where those truths about us must be known. Marriage is a layer of life that can only be explored in the context of a lifetime of commitment and sharing. Talking about the future with someone you have promised to share it with, no matter what, is a very different exercise from spinning dreams with friends or setting goals at work. A sexual relationship is different from a sexual act. The marriage bed that brings together all of the sharing that went on in the living room, the respect shown in mutual responsibility, the openness required for a good argument, the freedom from "performance anxiety," and the trust that comes from experience has satisfactions that graphic films and racy novels cannot convey. The unique level of commitment in a marriage allows the future to be more important than the past. This gives a confidence to the present that would be arrogance in any other relationship. For people committed to one another, the past can become a teacher rather than a weapon or a burden. Mistakes that are known, understood, and forgiven can be the foundation stones of a brilliant future. In the context of a marriage, "I am sorry" can turn into "I wish…" which can become "I hope…" which can become "We can…" Lifelong commitment establishes a future without limits and makes marriage a relationship with capabilities like no other.

In addition to all of this, it is fun to be married. Sex is fun. So are children and walks. Books, ball games, projects, plans, memories, mutual friends, movies, pets, houses, decisions, photos, families, meals, vacations, and conversations are especially enjoyable with someone you love. Sharing a warm bed or a cool drink, waking up beside someone and tip-toeing out without waking her, watching the stars come out or the seasons change, bringing home a surprise you know will delight or taking a step toward fulfilling a dream are wonderfully delightful. The private language lovers develop is bonding, but using its code in public when no one else knows what you are communicating is delicious. Winks and smiles, touches and taps, attentive ears and extended hands, praise that puffs you up, criticism that makes you better, someone you can laugh or cry or sing or dance with, and shared quiet are all combined uniquely in the fun of being together. Making up, being forgiven, caring when she is sick or when he is tired, finishing a list of chores, being generous or thoughtful, teaching and learning new things, thinking out loud and wondering are all part of the joy that makes all of the effort worthwhile.

There is an image that I have enjoyed for a long time. Marriage is like a child's drawing brought to a parent. The drawing itself may not be very good. The wise parent does not say what a splendid horse it is until he or she is certain that it is a horse. But when it is offered in love and received in love, it becomes a perfect picture. It goes on the refrigerator for all to see and many of them find a place in a box that is kept as a treasure long after the child has gone on to other things. Marriage is like that. Our efforts at being together may not be perfect. The wise spouse will take time to be sure what his or her partner is trying to say or do, and will not respond immediately to what seems to be presented. But when an effort is offered in love and received in love, it somehow becomes perfect. It is at least perfect enough to be held as a treasure while the rest of life goes on. Marriage is made to be like that. May yours be so crafted and responded to in love that what you do imperfectly is made perfect.

# ABOUT THE AUTHOR

Francis H. Wade, former Rector of St. Alban's Church, Washington, D.C. (1983-2005), has been a priest since 1966. He is now a lecturer, spiritual director, and writer.

A graduate of The Citadel and the Virginia Theological Seminary (M.Div. and D.Min.), Wade has served parishes in the dioceses of West Virginia and Washington. He and Mary Criss were married in 1963 and are the parents of two adult children.